Macbeth

WILLIAM SHAKESPEARE

Guide written by

Stewart Martin

A Letts EXPLORE Literature Guide

First published 1994
Reprinted 1994 twice, 1995, 1996, 1997 twice

Letts Educational
Aldine House
Aldine Place
London W12 8AW

This edition edited by Ron Simpson

Typeset by Jordan Publishing Design

Self-test questions devised by Claire Wright

Text design Jonathan Barnard

Text illustrations Hugh Marshall

Cover illustration Ivan Allen

British Library Cataloguing in Publication Data
A CIP record for this book is available from the British Library

ISBN 1 85758 247 0

Printed and bound in Great Britain
by Ashford Colour Press Ltd, Gosport, Hants

Letts Educational is the trading name of BPP (Letts Educational) Ltd

Contents

Plot synopsis

The action takes place in Scotland, technically in the 11th century, though there is little indication of period.

After Macbeth has triumphed in battle against the Norwegians and treacherous Scots, three witches predict that he will become king. Banquo, his fellow General, hears the prediction and also that his descendants will become kings. Macbeth's wife later persuades him to make the predictions come true by murdering the king.

Macbeth murders King Duncan when he visits Macbeth at his castle. Macbeth blames Duncan's guards for the murder and kills them, too. Duncan's sons escape and Macbeth tries to put the blame on them for bribing the guards to commit murder. Macbeth then declares himself King of Scotland.

Time passes and Macbeth's court is uneasy. Macbeth becomes afraid of Banquo for two reasons: his possible suspicions of Macbeth and the witches' prophecy that his descendants will become kings. Macbeth arranges for Banquo and his son, Fleance, to be murdered, but Fleance escapes. Banquo's ghost returns to haunt Macbeth.

Macbeth goes to see the witches to find out the future. They tell him to beware Macduff; that 'none of woman born' can harm him; and that he is safe until Birnam Wood comes to his castle. The witches also show a vision of the future with Banquo's heirs as kings.

Macbeth learns that Macduff has gone to England. Macbeth has Macduff's wife and children murdered. When Macduff hears about this, he becomes doubly determined to return to Scotland with Duncan's son, Malcolm, and overthrow and kill Macbeth.

Malcolm and Macduff lead a huge English army into Scotland, joining with Scottish Lords opposed to Macbeth. Macbeth learns that his wife, insane with guilt, is dead. His men desert him and his castle is captured. Macbeth, though desperate, still thinks he cannot be killed, but the witches have tricked him. Macduff was not born naturally. Macbeth says he will fight on anyway and Macduff kills him in hand-to-hand combat. Duncan's son, Malcolm, is hailed as the new King of Scotland.

Different editions of a Shakespeare play are usually very similar, although they may show occasional variation in spelling, punctuation, arrangement of scenes or lines, and even character names. However, you should have no difficulty in identifying the section being commented on in this Guide. The quotations and comments in this Guide are referenced to the New Penguin Shakespeare: you should note that the Penguin Popular Classics edition uses a slightly different text.

Who's who in *Macbeth*

Macbeth

In the beginning Macbeth is a successful general, described as noble and valiant. He kills the King of Scotland (Duncan) and the evil of this murder has powerful effects on him and the whole country. Macbeth knows that what he does is evil but the temptation is too strong and his ambition to be king gets the better of him. The witches play upon Macbeth's weakness and so does his ambitious wife Lady Macbeth. Macbeth thinks that the supernatural powers of the witches will help him but instead they lead him to his downfall. Macbeth's downfall is really his own fault, because he makes a deliberate choice to take the road to evil. He is responsible for the murder of King Duncan, his colleague Banquo, and Lady Macduff and her children.

At the end of the play Macbeth has changed from the 'Noble Macbeth' he was at the start, to a 'butcher' hated by everyone. Macbeth is, however, a strong character and is fully aware of the good he has rejected. This makes Macbeth a fascinating character because he is much more than just a horrible monster. It is possible to feel repelled by the evil in Macbeth and at the same time to feel sorry for the waste of all the good things in his character.

Because of the tight, compact structure of the play and the way everything centres on Macbeth, most of the other characters are not developed to any great degree and often serve merely to offset the main character.

Lady Macbeth

Lady Macbeth is Macbeth's wife. At the start of the play she seems to have a very strong character – stronger than Macbeth's – but by the end she is reduced to being afraid of the dark. At the beginning she is Macbeth's 'dearest partner of greatness', but at the end she is his 'fiend-like queen'.

The story of the play *Macbeth* is a bit like the story of the Garden of Eden, where Adam and Eve live happily until they are tempted away from goodness. Some people are reminded also of the Bible story of the angel Lucifer and how his pride and ambition led to God banishing him from heaven. If you see Macbeth as a good man who falls from grace, it is tempting to see Lady Macbeth as a traditional villainess, 'Eve' to Macbeth's 'Adam'. Certainly she has a lust for power and it is her goading that leads Macbeth to seize the throne of Scotland by murdering King Duncan.

On the other hand, Lady Macbeth cannot cope with the evil she has unleashed and she goes insane. Lady Macbeth is often seen as a symbol of evil like the witches, but at the end she falls victim to evil just like her husband. After the murder of King Duncan Macbeth increasingly shuts her out of his plans, so she becomes lonely and rather isolated. At the end of the play it is suggested that she commits suicide.

Banquo

Banquo is a loyal and honourable Scottish nobleman who is an impressive warrior in the king's army and Macbeth's friend. Banquo is with Macbeth when he first meets the witches, although they each react differently to what the witches have to say. Banquo senses that the witches are evil and is deeply suspicious of their powers. The witches predict that Banquo will father a line of rulers although he will not be one himself, and that he is 'Lesser than Macbeth, and greater'.

Banquo is Macbeth's close friend but later becomes one of his victims. After he has murdered King Duncan, Macbeth becomes afraid that Banquo's honesty may turn him into an enemy, so he has Banquo murdered. A question that remains unanswered about Banquo is whether this wise and moral man should – or could – have taken action when he realised that Macbeth was involved in the king's murder. Banquo's ghost haunts Macbeth with the continual reminder that Banquo's children will be the rightful monarchs.

Duncan

Duncan is the rightful King of Scotland who is murdered by Macbeth for his throne. He is noble, well-respected, dignified and appreciative of loyalty in others. Duncan is generous and trusting of the people around him – perhaps too trustful – especially of the two Thanes of Cawdor, both of whom betray him. Although we only see him in Act 1, Duncan is an important symbol of all the things which Macbeth overthrows and destroys.

Malcolm

King Duncan has two sons; Donalbain and Malcolm. Malcolm is named by his father as the next king. Like his father, he values bravery and loyalty, but unlike him he is aware that it is possible to trust people too much. Malcolm is quick to sense the danger after Duncan's murder and so, whilst his brother escapes to Ireland, he flees to England.

He has become shrewd and self-possessed by the time we meet him again later in England, when he tests Macduff's loyalty. He leads an army back to Scotland where, together with Macduff and other nobles, they defeat Macbeth. At the end of the play Malcolm makes a noble speech which seems designed to convince the audience that Scotland once again has its rightful king.

Macduff

Macduff believes Macbeth to be Duncan's murderer and does not consider him fit to be a king. He is a shrewd man who rejects belief in the powers of witchcraft. His conversation with Malcolm shows him to be honourable, loyal and patriotic and his reaction to the slaughter of his family reveals his tender feelings as husband and father.

Interestingly, Macduff takes little part in the action until the final stages, but the audience always senses that he is the man of honour who will oppose Macbeth. He is especially trusted by Duncan and discovers the body of the dead king. He immediately cuts himself off from any co-operation with Macbeth, avoiding the royal court and later refusing point-blank to attend the King. It comes as no surprise to the audience that the witches warn Macbeth about Macduff or that the Thane of Fife himself decides to flee to Malcolm in England: no doubt Macbeth's spies have found him out. When he returns, of course, he helps to secure the throne for Malcolm by slaying Macbeth in hand-to-hand combat.

The Macduff family

Lady Macduff and her son appear in only one brief scene, but you will notice that Shakespeare takes great care to make them sympathetic characters (though the clever remarks of the son may irritate in some performances!). Together they are a model affectionate family; they bravely stand up to the murderers; the son is more concerned about his mother's escape than his own death. Thus they provide the strongest reason for thinking Macbeth a 'butcher': who could have such good and innocent people destroyed? Remember, also, that there are others (children, servants) whose deaths we only hear of.

The witches

The witches are the physical embodiment of evil in the play. Like the serpent in the Garden of Eden, they represent temptation. The world of the witches is terrifying and their language is full of spitefulness, violence and grisly references to mutilation. Banquo senses that they are evil and he is very mistrustful of them. Macbeth is tempted by their predictions, because they echo his own thoughts. The witches never tell lies but, because they speak in puzzling riddles, it is possible for Macbeth to hear only what he wants to hear. By the time Macbeth realises his mistake in trusting them, it is too late.

In Shakespeare's day there was widespread belief in the supernatural world and the existence of witches, but people were also starting to question many of the older ideas about believing in supernatural things. This uncertainty is reflected in the play; we are never quite sure whether the witches have any real power or whether they can only persuade others or suggest things to them. The nature of the witches and their powers is ambiguous.

Hecat(e) and the **Three Other Witches** were certainly added to the play after Shakespeare's time, with their songs and dances. Hecat or Hecate (either spelling is acceptable) was the Queen of the Witches. Their appearances add nothing and the three extra witches are invariably cut in production, as Hecate often is.

The Scottish Lords

Apart from Banquo and Macduff, five characters are identified as Thanes of Scotland: **Lennox** (or Lenox), **Ross**, **Menteth** (or Menteith), **Angus** and **Caithness**. They have little individuality: as a group they tend to be loyal to Duncan, transfer their allegiance to King Macbeth and then rebel against him when things deteriorate too far. On stage Ross can be made an interesting character, as he is present at so many of the key events: the news of Macbeth's favour from Duncan, the discovery of Duncan's death, the royal banquet with Banquo's ghost, the murder of the Macduffs, the breaking of the news to Macduff, the final battles. He also seems disturbed at the events surrounding Duncan's death. His loyalties may be seen to change or sometimes to be concealed.

Servants

There are many characters who are employed as everything from Doctors to Messengers. Many lack individuality. The most interesting are:

The Porter: Shakespeare's acting company employed at least one clown who would expect a humorous role even in tragedies or history plays. *Macbeth* has very little humour, but the drunken porter is the clown's one chance for satirical comedy.

Seyton: The only named servant, Seyton remains loyal to Macbeth. As he first appears in Act 5, it is quite common in production to use Seyton for some of the earlier Messenger and Servant parts.

Murderers: The murderers of Banquo are ordinary men who have fallen on hard times: Macbeth persuades them that Banquo is to blame, though, almost certainly, Macbeth himself is. But who is the 'Third Murderer' who joins them with instructions from Macbeth and takes charge? This must be some trusted servant of Macbeth: surely not the King himself? More effective on stage is to expand the role of Seyton and use him as Macbeth's attendant and the Third Murderer.

The English

The English are presented in a flattering light, probably more to contrast with the darkness of Scotland than through national smugness. The King (Edward the Confessor) is praised and **Seyward** (or Siward), Earl of Northumberland, and his son, represent nobility and courage. This is one of many father/son relationships in the play: the Macduffs, Banquo and Fleance, Duncan and his two sons (Donalbain a very shadowy character). Between them the King, old Seyward and young Seyward provide a chain of loyalty and responsibility, in nation and family, that contrasts with the situation in Scotland.

Chorus

In Greek tragedy the Chorus (a group of individually anonymous characters) commented on the action, telling of events off-stage, judging the wisdom and morality of the main characters, warning what might happen. Shakespeare used a character called 'Chorus' in some plays for the same purpose. In *Macbeth* there are several characters who have no real individuality, who make one appearance in a choric role. The **Old Man** in Act 2, Scene 4, and the **Gentlewoman** in Act 5, Scene 1, are good examples.

Themes and images in *Macbeth*

Themes are the important ideas that run through the play. You will come across them often. They connect the story, the characters and the different scenes in the play.

When words and descriptions suggest a picture in your mind, it is called an **image**. Images are often used to make an idea stronger, or to encourage you to think of things from a particular point of view. If you described someone as being 'as thin as a rake' or as behaving 'like a wild animal' you would be using simple images.

Shakespeare was a great writer who used themes and images a great deal. You will find many very striking and impressive examples. Others will be less obvious, so you need to pay careful attention to the language that Shakespeare has used. Read the following notes carefully.

Ambition

Ambition

Both Macbeth and Lady Macbeth are ambitious. Lady Macbeth is single-minded in persuading Macbeth to kill King Duncan, so that he will become king. At first Macbeth is unwilling to give in to ambition, but the witches and Lady Macbeth tempt him. The result is a disaster and Macbeth loses everything. He finds that being king gives him no satisfaction. One of the play's main themes is that when people allow their sense of what is right to be overcome by their ambition, they are doomed to disaster.

Clothing

Clothing

If you wear someone else's clothes they may feel uncomfortable and get in your way. The robes of kingship do not fit Macbeth: he is not worthy of them because he has taken the rightful king's throne. He is never comfortable as king and is keen to get back into his armour at the end of the play partly because of the imminent battle, but also because armour is his natural clothing. Macbeth's proper place in the world is as a loyal soldier and when he leaves this position, disaster follows.

The idea of Macbeth's wearing 'borrowed robes' keeps appearing in the play. There are other references to 'cloaking' as in covering or hiding something and the word 'rapt' is used as a pun, to mean 'absorbed' or 'enchanted' as well as 'wrapped' (concealed or shrouded).

Chaos

Chaos

A sense of chaos and disorder runs through the play. In the first scene the witches chant that 'Fair is foul, and foul is fair' and this paradox sets the tone. Macbeth cannot tell whether the witches are on his side or not and his murder of the king plunges the country into turmoil.

Chaos and disorder are suggested in many ways. Birds of prey, toads and snakes suggest a threatening atmosphere. Nature is turned upside down after King Duncan's murder, when hawks are killed by their prey and Duncan's horses eat each other. Blood often seems to run through the story. Thunder, lightning, storms and shipwrecks are connected with the witches and the influence of evil in the world. Howling and shrieking seem to follow Macbeth. He is forever in a hurry, spurred on by his ambition. He cannot stand uncertainty, waiting or inaction, and has little patience. The theme of chaos is related in this way to that of time.

Light and dark

Light and dark

Images of light are connected to a state of innocence and purity. King Duncan says that the signs of nobility are 'like stars'. Light is a symbol of truth, openness and goodness in the world.

Macbeth and Lady Macbeth are creatures of the dark because darkness symbolises treachery, cruelty and evil. Macbeth tells the stars to hide their fires and Lady Macbeth calls up the blackest smoke of Hell to hide her actions. Towards the end of the play, when Lady Macbeth is overcome by guilt, she fears the dark and has to have a candle next to her all night.

Order

Order

People in Shakespeare's time thought that every person and thing had a natural place, decided by God. Macbeth's main crime is in upsetting this natural order. He murders people so that they die before their time. He throws the political stability of Scotland into chaos and destroys his marriage and his own mental 'order'. His wife actually goes mad, breaking natural order again by taking her own life.

In the play, loyalty to the true king and the State is shown as good, rebellion against it as bad. Growth is seen as a symbol of order: there are references to the 'planting' of seeds and of people, to seeds germinating and to the goodness of things growing naturally, especially children. Under Macbeth, Scotland becomes 'drowned with weeds' and he fears the children of King Duncan, Macduff and Banquo because they have the potential to grow into something that could destroy his evil world.

Sleep

Sleep

Sleep is described in the play as a gift from nature and the ability to sleep well is connected with innocence. After he has murdered King Duncan, Macbeth says that he has 'murdered sleep' by what he has done, and is tormented by nightmares. Lady Macbeth walks in her sleep and repeatedly acts out the murder of the king.

Evil

Evil

The nature and effects of evil dominate the action of the play. The potential for evil is present in nature, in man and in animals and the play's imagery evokes this.

Evil is a supernatural force, manifested in the shape of the three witches whose successful temptation of Macbeth threatens to plunge the world back into the chaos from which, as the Elizabethans supposed, God released it, when he created order and morality.

Time

Time

Macbeth is continually aware of time. Before Duncan's murder he speaks of being 'upon this banked shoal of time' – between the past and the future – 'jumping the life to come' and escaping retribution. The midnight bell is the cue for Duncan's death. The future, with the question of the royal succession, obsesses him. He plots the murder of Lady Macduff with 'Time, thou anticipat'st my dread exploits.' When his wife dies, he says: 'She should have died hereafter' and contemplates the empty future stretching away with 'tomorrow and tomorrow and tomorrow....'

Essays

In the section on **Coursework essays**, possible subjects for your coursework assignments are analysed. In the main **Text commentary**, the **Essays icon** marks material that will be of particular use for these coursework assignments; in each case the essay subject is identified and a relevant comment or quotation added.

Text commentary

Act 1 Scene 1

The play starts with thunder, lightning and the three witches.

The witches

The witches

By starting the play with the witches and with thunder and lightning, Shakespeare leaves you in no doubt about what it is going to be about. It is going to be about the struggle between the forces of good and the forces of evil; a struggle between the light and the darkness.

It is also clear who is to be the target for the forces of evil: the witches make an appointment to meet again to lure Macbeth to destruction.

The supernatural

Note how Shakespeare instantly creates a mood of terror and unearthly evil: the first stage direction, 'Thunder and lightning. Enter Three Witches'.

Chaos

When the witches chant 'Fair is foul, and foul is fair:/Hover through the fog and filthy air' you can guess that it is going to be hard in the play to tell the difference between good and evil. The way things appear may not be the way they really are. Things that look good may turn out to be evil, evil things may seem to be good; just like some characters in the play.

Grey-Malkin and Padock are the witches' familiars, demon-companions in animal form. It is usually thought that Grey-Malkin is a cat, Padock a toad.

Act 1 Scene 2

The Captain tells Duncan about the bravery of Macbeth and Banquo. They are in command of the army that is fighting off an invasion. King Duncan is grateful and makes Macbeth Thane (Lord) of Cawdor.

A different view of Macbeth

Duncan

King Duncan's first words in the play are: 'What bloody man is that?' Duncan is referring to the Captain who is bleeding because he has come straight from battle. The image of spilled blood appears a lot in the play. It is ironic that Duncan should mention it first. Macbeth is ambitious to become king and will soon make a 'bloody man' out of Duncan.

The loyalty and bravery of Macbeth and Banquo are contrasted with the treason and cowardice of the Thane of Cawdor, who betrayed the king and joined the enemy. The Captain says that Macbeth and Banquo were savage in battle. Macbeth's savagery is praised here because it has preserved the rightful king. Later on, Macbeth's savage character is condemned as evil and his viciousness overthrows the king and creates chaos in the land.

Macbeth and Banquo

Macbeth

Images of blood are often connected with images about water in the play. Here Macbeth and Banquo are said to 'bathe in reeking wounds'. The idea of bathing is connected here not with water, but with blood. The Captain says it was as if they were trying to 'memorise another Golgotha'. Golgotha ('the place of the skull') was where Christ was crucified. Later in the play Banquo will 'bathe in blood' and Macbeth will describe the blood he has shed as a river.

This scene gives a glowing picture of Macbeth and Banquo as loyal and brave. When the treacherous Thane of Cawdor is captured, the king says he must be executed, and gives his title to Macbeth. The irony is that the new Thane of Cawdor will be even more treacherous.

Two armies

Characters

'...brave Macbeth – well he deserves that name...', 'Noble Macbeth!'. Can this be evil monster who nearly destroys his country?

Apparently Macbeth and Banquo have triumphed over two armies: that of the rebel Macdonwald and that of the Norwegian king, Sweno, assisted by the traitor Cawdor. As in Act 5 (when Macbeth is the king under attack) there is a union of discontented Scots and a foreign army. This double triumph enables the scene to be structured around two great 'messenger's speeches', full of ornate vocabulary and images and praising Macbeth's valour: the first by the Captain, the second by Ross. Note the words, images and comparisons used to glorify Macbeth. If you make a list, 'Bellona's bridegroom' could come at the top; that means 'husband of the goddess of war' and suggests that Macbeth is worthy to be considered a God of War.

Act 1 Scene 3

Macbeth and Banquo are returning from the battle and meet the three witches who predict that Macbeth will be king and that Banquo will be the father of many kings.

The story about the Pilot's thumb

Chaos

Sleep

One of the witches describes how she will punish a sailor (the Pilot) because his wife would not give her some of the chestnuts she was eating. This shows how spiteful the witches are and how they can do a lot of harm. The witch is not powerful enough to sink the ship, but she can make sure it is tossed about in stormy seas, and will torment the Pilot so that he cannot sleep. The ship is a metaphor (a figure of speech) for the ship of state and represents Scotland, which is going to suffer a 'storm' when Macbeth is its Pilot. The witches can only create the climate for evil: man alone causes chaos in the world by destroying order.

Our first meeting with Macbeth and Banquo

Macbeth

As is the case with King Duncan, the first words spoken by Macbeth are very significant. He enters to the sound of a beating drum and says that he has never seen 'so foul and fair a day', meaning that the battle has been foul but their victory has been splendid. Notice how his words echo those spoken earlier by the witches. Why? Perhaps the witches knew he would say these words and were mocking him. Perhaps the witches have some control over him. Perhaps Shakespeare is suggesting that Macbeth and the witches are similar in character as well as in the way they talk.

The witches' predictions

The witches

Clothing

The witches' words have a powerful effect on Macbeth. Banquo notices this and asks him if he fears their words. Banquo cannot see why this great warrior should be afraid, when he is promised only good things. What the witches say seems to strike a chord in Macbeth's mind, especially the prediction that he will be king.

Banquo introduces clothing as one of the major images in the play. The pun is on 'rapt' meaning 'totally involved in' and 'wrapped' meaning 'covered' or 'enveloped in'. Banquo also calls on the witches to tell him his future and they say he will be the father of kings.

The witches vanish and Macbeth wonders if they have disappeared into the air: what he thought was solid has melted away. Other things around Macbeth that he thinks are solid, like his friends, loyalty, a good king on the throne and law and order in the state, will also melt away under the evil influence of the witches.

Banquo

Banquo seems suspicious of the witches. Unlike Macbeth, he has no hidden ambitions. Macbeth seems worried about the prediction that Banquo's children will be kings, as though this is some kind of threat to his future. If Banquo's children will be kings, Macbeth's rise to power will be pointless if his line stops when he dies.

The new Thane of Cawdor

Clothing

Soon after the witches vanish, Ross and Angus arrive with the news that Macbeth has been given the title Thane of Cawdor. Macbeth is amazed and asks them why they 'dress him in borrowed robes'. Soon he will be wearing the stolen clothes of the king.

Macbeth says that 'the greatest is behind', meaning that all he has to achieve now is to become king. He makes another mention of Banquo's children being kings and the idea seems to affect him.

Banquo advises caution, pointing out that the forces of evil sometimes tell people small things that will come true so that they can deceive them into believing greater things which are false. Banquo recognises the witches for what they are and for the moment puts them out of his mind. Look, however, at how Macbeth reacts.

Macbeth in turmoil

Guilt

'Horrid image'/'horrible imaginings' – nearly identical phrases, but whose imagination: Macbeth's or the Witches'?

Macbeth

Macbeth speaks his first major soliloquy. A soliloquy is a speech in which a character speaks directly to the audience and gives insight into his or her inner thoughts. Macbeth asks himself two questions. If what the witches said was evil, why have two good things they said turned out to be true – he *was* Thane of Glamis and *is* now Thane of Cawdor. If what the witches said was good, why does his body react so violently to their predictions? Notice that it is Macbeth who mentions 'murder', whereas the witches said nothing about murdering anyone. It is Macbeth who connects the ideas of kingship and murder. But at the moment Macbeth thinks the idea of murder is 'fantastical', meaning that it exists only in his imagination. Macbeth decides to leave it to chance whether he will become king or not.

Clothing

Banquo again talks about Macbeth being 'rapt', this time in thought. He wonders if, perhaps Macbeth's new title – Thane of Cawdor – feels strange at the moment. Banquo supposes that Macbeth will get used to his new honours and will feel more comfortable wearing them.

Banquo, it seems, is less impressed with the truth of the witches' predictions. Look at his speech beginning 'That trusted home...' (lines 119–125 in the Penguin edition) and note how he can see through the trickery of the witches and also Macbeth's motives in asking him whether he hopes his heirs will become kings.

Macbeth's speeches

Throughout this scene it is fascinating to note when Macbeth speaks and when he is silent; how he speaks to different people. With the witches he is firstly struck dumb and then urgent in calling after them. You should examine his speeches after Ross and Angus give the great news. His speeches are of three types: aside (that is, his thoughts, told in soliloquy to the audience), to Banquo only and to everyone. Note where he does not speak (during the asides he is silent to his companions), what his thoughts are and how far they dominate his speeches to Banquo alone.

> By now you should be clear about the part that **the witches** play in setting events in motion. Their suggestion that Macbeth will become king plays on his secret ambition leading him to do terrible crimes that will affect all Scotland. Images of blood and water suggest that blood can be justly shed only in the service of the state and therefore in support of order. The image of clothing has been introduced: clothes may be worn to hide what is really there, or may not fit because they do not belong to the wearer. The character of the person inside may not match the outside appearance. You have met **Banquo** and seen him as a comrade of Macbeth. Banquo is aware of how evil the witches could be and the danger involved in believing what they say. **Macbeth** is admired for his bravery in battle and for his loyalty to the king. You have been given a brief glimpse into his thoughts through his soliloquy and you know that, although he is ambitious to be king, he seems to be content to let chance take its course.

Act 1 Scene 4

Macbeth and Banquo arrive at King Duncan's court.

Duncan

King Duncan says to Macbeth that he has started to 'plant' him, meaning that he will make sure that Macbeth grows greater and stronger as a reward for his service. This is ironic because what is growing in Macbeth is the seed of his ambition to be king himself. When this seed grows it will lead to Duncan's death.

Macbeth changes his mind

King Duncan says that his eldest son, Malcolm, is to succeed him as king. It was the custom in Scotland for each king to be elected by the Thanes. Duncan's action is therefore unusual and, to Macbeth in particular, provocative. This announcement therefore comes as a shock to Macbeth, who has only recently decided to leave to chance whether or not he becomes king himself.

Evil

Macbeth changes his mind because he now sees Duncan's son Malcolm as an obstacle between himself and the throne. Macbeth makes a short speech as an 'aside', a short soliloquy telling the audience his thoughts. He admits that he has 'black and deep desires' and calls upon the stars not to shine their light on his thoughts.

To show his gratitude to Macbeth, the king says he will visit him at his castle. This is a great honour for Macbeth. It is ironic that fate seems to have given Macbeth the perfect opportunity to fulfil his ambition. He rushes to his castle to prepare for his honoured guest.

Act 1 Scene 5

Lady Macbeth reads a letter from Macbeth, telling her about the meeting with the witches and Duncan's forthcoming visit. Lady Macbeth vows to kill the king and to persuade Macbeth to join her.

The letter

Macbeth's letter is highly revealing. His version of events is accurate, but you should note that the events which he chooses to report to her all point towards the possible seizure of the throne. 'I have learnt by the perfectest report they have in them more than mortal knowledge' means that he is sure they are right. His wife is 'his dearest partner of greatness' (power/supremacy), 'greatness is promised' her. Macbeth may have pangs of conscience, Lady Macbeth may drive him on, but you should have no doubt who first has the idea of seizing power.

Lady Macbeth considers her husband's character

Lady Macbeth is delighted with her husband's letter. Although she knows her husband is ambitious, she says he lacks ruthlessness, while she herself will stop at nothing. She says that this ruthlessness is an 'illness' (i.e. evil) that Macbeth doesn't have, saying that Macbeth will take any opportunity that comes his way, but he only wants to win his honours honestly. He wants to be king even though the throne is not his by right, but he will not play falsely. Lady Macbeth decides that she will have to help him to find the necessary determination.

Lady Macbeth and the witches' predictions

Lady Macbeth

A messenger comes to tell Lady Macbeth that King Duncan will arrive that night. Lady Macbeth is excited, seeing this as the perfect opportunity to make Macbeth king. She calls up the spirits of darkness to take away her natural womanliness and to fill her instead with the worst of bitterness, wickedness and cruelty. She does not want any natural feelings of regret or conscience to get in the way of what she intends.

Characters

'...unsex me here/And fill me from the crown to the toe top-full/Of direst cruelty.'

Clothing

Like Macbeth she asks the powers of darkness to hide her thoughts so that not even the forces of heaven can see through the 'blanket of the dark'. This is another example of the clothing image, this time meaning cloaking or hiding something, so that its true nature is concealed.

When Macbeth arrives to tell her that Duncan is coming to stay that night but will leave the next day, Lady Macbeth predicts that Duncan will never see another day's sunrise. Her plans are already made.

Macbeth

She tells Macbeth to deceive their guest and to hide his real thoughts. She says that people can read Macbeth's thoughts in his face. She tells him to be more like the poisonous serpent that lies hidden beneath the innocent flower. She says that Macbeth must become better at deceiving people and at being evil, if he wants to achieve his ambitions.

Lady Macbeth's power of deception shows even in talking to her husband, where she uses phrases with more than one meaning. What does 'He that's coming/Must be provided for' mean?

Act 1 Scene 6

King Duncan arrives at Macbeth's castle with his followers. Lady Macbeth welcomes him.

When King Duncan arrives at Macbeth's castle he and Banquo talk about how pleasant a place it is to visit. They say the air 'recommends itself' and 'is delicate'. This is ironic in view of Lady Macbeth's words in the previous scene, and even more so when compared with what the witches said about the 'fog and filthy air' surrounding their evil deeds. Lady Macbeth's words to Duncan are false, but she has no difficulty in hiding her real thoughts.

Lady Macbeth's concealment of her motives and feelings is all part of a very formal little scene: everybody is polite and complimentary. Lady Macbeth is the great deceiver, of course, but is Banquo as happy to be there as he suggests? Macbeth is already in the castle, as we know and as Duncan says. Why is he not there to welcome Duncan?

Act 1 Scene 7

Macbeth keeps changing his mind about killing the king. He is finally persuaded to go ahead by the determination of Lady Macbeth.

In his second major soliloquy Macbeth tells the audience about the doubts and fears which torment him.

Macbeth considers his options

Guilt

'This even-handed justice/Commends the ingredience of our poisoned chalice/To our own lips.'

Macbeth cannot make up his mind whether to kill Duncan. He wrestles with his conscience. He says that if the murder could be done quickly, without the inevitable consequences, then he should do it quickly. He knows that the murder would be wrong and that he would end up paying the price for his crime. Macbeth is a decisive man of action, but this is a moral problem and it makes him hesitate. Macbeth lists reasons why he should not kill the king. He is his kinsman, his host and his subject: Macbeth should therefore be the one to protect him.

Macbeth's conscience is very persuasive. He tells himself that Duncan's goodness and kindness is such that his killing would provoke a tremendous outcry. Duncan's goodness will be 'like angels, trumpet-tongued' if he is murdered, and Macbeth will be condemned to 'deep damnation'. Notice how images of heaven and hell are linked to the action of the play here – because Duncan is the rightful King, heaven would be outraged at his murder.

However, heaven and hell are not Macbeth's only (or, even, main) concern. His conscience may plague him, but his main worry is with 'this bank and shoal of time': the here and now. Duncan may be saintly, Macbeth may risk damnation, but he is prepared to 'jump' (risk) the life to come if he can get away with it in this life. The problem is that the murderer of a king creates a precedent and risks the same thing happening to him – as it does to Macbeth.

Ambition

Macbeth admits that the only thing driving him on is his selfish ambition. Rather as Lady Macbeth did, he worries that his ambition may be greater than his ability to achieve it. He may be like a horseman who tries to vault too hastily onto his horse's back and finishes up falling off on the other side.

Macbeth changes his mind again

Clothing

When Lady Macbeth comes in he tells her he will not murder Duncan. He says that Duncan has given him 'new honours' lately and that he wants to enjoy the 'golden' opinion of everyone. He wants to 'wear' his honours whilst they are new. He sees himself 'dressed' in the good opinions of other people. Why does Macbeth give his wife these reasons and not those he has just been giving to himself? Perhaps he does not want to admit that he has a conscience and is unhappy about doing evil. Perhaps he does not want to seem weak.

Lady Macbeth persuades Macbeth

Lady Macbeth

Lady Macbeth continues the use of clothing imagery, but turns it against Macbeth. She says that he is acting as if he were drunk when he clothed himself in his hopes to be king. She accuses him of being a coward. In a powerful speech she explains how far she would be prepared to go to get what she wanted. She tells him that if, like him, she had sworn to do something, then, before she would go back on her word, she would pluck her own baby from sucking milk at her nipple and dash its brains out.

Evil

Lady Macbeth seems to have joined the forces of evil. She has seen a chance to make her husband king and is determined not to let it slip away. She is very forceful in her language and conjures up images of horror. She seems to have been granted her earlier wish to the evil spirits to 'fill me from the crown to the toe top-full of direst cruelty'.

Macbeth once more changes his mind

Macbeth

Macbeth's earlier decision not to kill Duncan crumbles under the scornful attack of his wife, especially when his bravery is questioned. But he is still worried about what will happen to them if they fail. Lady Macbeth tells him that they will not fail if he keeps his nerve.

She tells Macbeth the details of her plan and he admires her determination. He says that she should have only male children so that they would have all her courage and strength of character.

What is a man?

Manhood is a frequent theme in this scene. Lady Macbeth sees it simply: a man has courage to act and to face danger. Macbeth (lines 47–48) says that he dares to do anything that is suitable to a man; to do more would be unmanly. What does he mean by this? What other qualities might manhood involve?

At the end of Scene 3 Macbeth was going to leave it to chance to determine whether he became king or not. By now he has decided that he will kill the king and seize his throne. You should be clear about why this change has taken place.

Lady Macbeth's part in persuading Macbeth to kill the king has been crucial. Her ruthless determination to make Macbeth king has overcome all his doubts. But what has happened to the earlier Macbeth, who was a noble, brave and loyal subject of the rightful king? You know he is a man of great bravery, even of savagery on the battlefield. When he is not on the battlefield, however, he seems a different man.

Macbeth knows the difference between right and wrong, as you saw from his reaction to the witches' predictions. He is ambitious, but he also enjoys the good opinion which the king and other people have of him. His conscience is troubled by what will happen if he gives in to his ambitions. He is clear about all the reasons for not killing the king and about the evil consequences that might follow if he does. However, he is tempted by the witches' predictions, which seem to be coming true. His better judgement is then overcome by his wife's fierce accusations about his lack of courage and by the strength of her determination to have him crowned. The evil consequences of his 'vaulting ambition' will soon appear.

Self-test questions Act One

Uncover the plot

Delete two of the three alternatives given, to find the correct plot. Beware possible misconceptions and muddles.

Macbeth, Thane of Fife/Cawdor/Glamis, is reported to have fought bravely against the King of England/Norway/Sweden, and is awarded the title of the treacherous Ross/Cawdor/Siward. Returning with Banquo/Ross/Angus, he is hailed by three murderers/thanes/witches under his new title – and also as 'prosperous gentleman'/ 'not so happy'/'king hereafter': his companion is told that Macbeth's heirs/ Duncan's heirs/Banquo's heirs will also be kings. The present King Duncan/ Malcolm/Edward invites himself to Macbeth's castle – already called a 'fatal entrance' by Lady Macbeth/Macbeth/Banquo. Lady Macbeth/Macbeth/Banquo wrestles between conscience and ambition, but is spurred to action by Macbeth/Lady Macbeth/Banquo's challenges. They will use the daggers of Duncan's sons/porters/chamberlains for the deed.

Who? What? Where? Why? How?

1 Who is named as Duncan's successor, and what title is he given?

2 Who are 'the instruments of darkness'?
3 What titles does Macbeth hold by the end of Act 1 – and what titles has he been promised?
4 What is unnatural about the witches' appearance?
5 Where is Macbeth's castle?
6 Where do the witches first meet Macbeth and Banquo?
7 Why does Lady Macbeth say: 'Yet I do fear thy nature'?
8 Why is Macbeth reluctant to kill Duncan – according to his words to himself, and to Lady Macbeth?
9 How does Lady Macbeth propose to deal with Duncan's guards?
10 How does the witches' curse on the master of the Tiger parallel Macbeth's own future?

Who said that?

1 Who says: 'And oftentimes to win us to our harm/The instruments of darkness tell us truths'?
2 Who says: 'And fill me, from the crown to the toe, top-full/Of direst cruelty'?
3 Who says, and of whom: 'His virtues/Will plead like angels, trumpet-tongu'd, against/The deep damnation of his taking off'?
4 Who says 'He was a gentleman on whom I built an absolute trust', of whom and why is this ironic?
5 Who says: 'Art thou afeard/To be the same in thine own act and valour/As thou art in desire?', to whom, and why?

Open quotes

Find the line – and complete the phrase or sentence.

1 'Stars, hide your fires…'
2 'Thou wouldst be great…'
3 'That but this blow/Might be the be-all...'
4 'I have no spur…'
5 'We fail!…'

Parallel lines

In a play full of prophecies, ironies and images, you'll find many echoes. Where do you find an echo of the following lines – and what is the effect created?

1 The witches prophesy that Macbeth will come 'when the battle's lost and won'.
2 The witches say: 'Fair is foul, and foul is fair'.
3 Macbeth, hailed as Cawdor, asks: 'Why do you dress me/In borrowed robes?' (THREE echoes...)
4 Duncan says: 'Signs of nobleness, like stars, shall shine/On all deservers'.
5 Banquo, uncertain as to the witches' sex, says: 'You should be women...'

Imperfect speakers?

The witches are called 'imperfect speakers' because their meaning seems ambiguous. Later they are called 'equivocators'. Here are some early signs that ambiguity and lack of trust are major themes in the play.

1 What three apparently contradictory promises do the witches make to Banquo?
2 Why might the audience already be uneasy when the witches hail Macbeth by three titles?
3 What does Banquo suspect, when the first prophecy proves true?
4 Why does Macbeth think 'This supernatural soliciting/Cannot be ill; cannot be good'?

Act 2 Scene 1

We are at Macbeth's castle. Whilst alone at night on the battlements, Macbeth sees a vision of a dagger.

Briefly alone on the battlements with his son Fleance, Banquo's concerns and suspicions are evident. There is an edginess about his conversation (does he draw his sword?) and he talks of his 'cursed thoughts' that will not let him sleep: not the only insomniac in the play by any means! What are these 'cursed thoughts': worries about the witches or suspicions of how Macbeth is reacting to the prophecies?

Banquo

Macbeth arrives and he and Banquo talk about the predictions of the witches. Banquo reminds Macbeth that the witches showed some of the truth to him. Macbeth now puts on the 'false face' his wife talked about and says that he has not thought about the witches' predictions at all. You know that this is not true.

Macbeth sees the dagger

After Banquo and Fleance leave him, Macbeth sees a vision of a dagger covered in blood, with the handle pointing towards him. Macbeth speaks another important soliloquy. He wonders whether the dagger is inviting him to do the murder. His mind is full of dark thoughts and this fearless soldier is now tormented by images of blood and fear of the unknown.

Chaos

This kind of killing goes against Macbeth's nature and against natural law. Notice how Macbeth says that across half the world (the half in the darkness of night) nature 'seems dead'. The darkness is a symbol of the way evil powers are rising up to strike at the powers of goodness and light. Macbeth wonders whether he is going insane.

Imagery

The 'fatal vision' of the dagger (**The supernatural**) is one of many uses of the blood imagery, literally ('gouts of blood') and metaphorically ('the bloody business').

The dagger is the first of several visions shown to Macbeth. He cannot tell whether they are real or imaginary. They are symbols of the power of evil spirits in the world and of the evil that is growing in his own heart. As the bell rings, he goes to do the murder.

Why does Macbeth do it?

Characters

Is Macbeth a cold-blooded killer? 'This is a sorry sight'/'I had most need of blessing'/'I'll go no more... Look on't again I dare not.'

Macbeth

You have seen that Macbeth is a great warrior who is used to making life-and-death decisions in battle. But here he is torn between doing the murder or not doing it. Eventually he decides to go and do it. Maybe this is because he really is an evil man. Maybe he is so mixed up that he cannot sort out the difference between right and wrong. Perhaps he is under the power of the witches. Maybe he does not really know what to do and is acting on the spur of the moment, without really thinking too much. Try to work out for yourself why he finally decides to do the murder. There are several possible reasons and different people might come to different conclusions. It depends partly on what sort of people you think the different characters are. Make up your own mind from what has gone on in the play so far.

Act 2 Scene 2

It is night-time. Lady Macbeth waits anxiously for Macbeth as he murders Duncan. They rush back to bed when they hear loud knocking at the castle gate.

Lady Macbeth

Until now Lady Macbeth has seemed very determined and strong. Here she is very much on edge. Although earlier she seemed able to do the most terrible deeds, now she explains that she could not carry out the murder herself because the sleeping Duncan reminded her of her father. This is the first sign of Lady Macbeth's conscience and feelings of guilt. She, too, seems to realise the wrongness of the murder.

Macbeth has murdered sleep

Macbeth comes in and says he has killed Duncan as he slept. Sleep represents innocence and peace and Macbeth imagines he has also murdered these. Duncan's innocent servants can say 'Amen' in their prayers, but Macbeth cannot. He is terrified because he knows that he can never be forgiven for his crime. Lady Macbeth says these worries are 'brain-sickly'.

Lady Macbeth

Lady Macbeth has been the organiser of the murder from the outset and here, once she has again taken charge of herself, she clears up behind Macbeth's bunglings. She 'drugged the possets' of the grooms sleeping in the outer chamber; she laid the daggers ready; all Macbeth had to do was the deed itself.

Now here he is with two blood-stained daggers which should have been left with the grooms, the supposed murderers.

Imagery

More blood – and note how Shakespeare links it with **Guilt**: 'I'll gild (paint) the faces of the grooms withal (with the blood)/For it must seem their guilt.'

The terrified Macbeth is incapable of returning to the murder scene, so Lady Macbeth does so, smearing the grooms with blood. On her return she finds Macbeth transfixed with thoughts of blood and guilt and once again takes charge of the situation. She tells Macbeth to go and wash the blood from his hands. She means the visible blood on his hands, but Macbeth fears for his blood-stained soul. You should compare this with her behaviour in the sleepwalking scene at the start of Act 5.

Sleep

Sleep is described here as 'chief nourisher in life's feast'. Sleep and food are seen as essential parts of nature. Both are needed for life. Macbeth has destroyed this natural order and this is seen again later, when he destroys the calm and order of his own coronation banquet.

The language of guilt

Shakespeare conveys Macbeth's feelings of guilt not only in what he says, but in how he says it. Most striking in this scene is that his speeches keep turning in on themselves, constantly returning to a word or a phrase. 'Amen', for instance ('So be it', the traditional end of a prayer), is never out of his thoughts, though he cannot say it and mean it.

Imagery

A different image here, one that will forever symbolise the Macbeths' **Guilt**: 'Macbeth does murder sleep'. How often does Macbeth return to that image here? And what does that show of **Character**?

Notice, at this stage, that Macbeth is not hardened to his crimes; that comes later, as murder leads to murder.

Banquo says in Act 2 Sc 1 that all the lights in heaven are out, meaning that the stars are blacked out. The whole of Act 2 takes place in darkness. The darkness is a symbol of the evil which Duncan's murder casts over the whole world.

Scenes 1 and 2 cover the murder of King Duncan. Macbeth pretends to his friend Banquo that he has not thought about the predictions of the witches. **Banquo** has been having bad dreams, but has prayed to heaven for help. Banquo fights the temptation to believe the witches but Macbeth gives way to it. So Macbeth does not know whether the dagger that appears is real or only in his mind.

Macbeth decides to kill Duncan. We see a big difference between his and his wife's behaviour now. Macbeth carries out the murder but is almost hysterical afterwards. In contrast, **Lady Macbeth** seems weak and is a frightened bundle of nerves when Macbeth is doing the murder but is calm and organised afterwards. Macbeth is a man of action but is confused when he loses his sense of right and wrong. Lady Macbeth feels no guilt about persuading Macbeth to murder the king, but she cannot murder him herself.

Act 2 Scene 3

The castle's Porter (night watchman) answers the knocking at the gate. Macduff has come to wake the king, but discovers his dead body instead. During the panic and confusion that results, Duncan's sons decide to escape to safety.

The Porter

The comical Porter adds nothing to the plot, but this is not his purpose. Shorter scenes in the play are either a reminder of what has happened so far or a preparation for what is coming. This scene is light-hearted and relieves the tension of the last scene as well as contrasting with the next, when Duncan's murder is discovered.

The gateway to Hell

The Porter imagines he is the gatekeeper in Hell. This was a traditional figure in plays before Shakespeare's time but it has a special importance here. Macbeth's castle has, in a way, become the gateway to Hell. The Porter makes jokes about the perils of drink and about having too much of a good thing; about a farmer who is ruined because of his ambition; about people who destroy themselves because they confuse truth with half-truths (they 'equivocate' between the truth and lies); and about a tailor who was hanged for stealing precious fabric.

Evil

In some ways the Porter's jokes tell us something about Macbeth, who you might feel is also confused; he too has become corrupted (drunk) with evil, will be ruined by having too much ambition, believes too much in the witches' half-truths and he has 'stolen' the king's crown.

Certainly the Porter gives a satirical picture of a dishonest world. What with treachery and lying and unnatural events such as Lennox recounts (and Ross and the Old Man in Scene 4), is it any surprise that people like Macbeth rise to be kings?

A rough night

Duncan

Macduff and Lennox have come to wake the king. They describe the storm during the night. The description of the storm is symbolic of the effect that Duncan's murder is already having on the world around. The murder of the king has filled the night with screams of death and other portents. Notice how sickness seems to have infected even the earth itself, when Lennox says that he has heard that the earth 'was feverous and did shake'. Macbeth agrees ironically that ''twas a rough night'.

The murder is discovered

Chaos

Sleep

Notice the imagery which Macduff uses when he tells the others that he has found Duncan murdered. This goes beyond the mere facts about the murder. The murder has unleashed chaos (confusion) on the world and is sacrilegious (against God). Macduff says that to look at the murdered body will 'destroy your sight with a new Gorgon'. (The Gorgons were female Greek monsters with live snakes for hair, huge teeth and brass claws, and the ability to turn to stone all who looked on them. Note that the only women you have met so far in the play are the witches and Lady Macbeth.)

Macduff describes sleep as an imitation ('counterfeit') of death and tells Banquo to rise up like a 'sprite' (a ghost) from its 'grave' (his bed) to look at 'this horror'. Later in the play Banquo's ghost rises from the dead to visit another 'horror' when it returns to haunt Macbeth.

Macbeth pretends that life now has no meaning for him

Chaos

Time

Images of blood and water appear again in Macbeth's speech 'Had I but died an hour before this…', which you should read carefully. It is a prophetic speech. Death does become unimportant to Macbeth and he is indeed no longer 'blessed'. Decide whether you think Macbeth is just saying these words because he feels that the others expect him to say something like this or whether you think he really means them.

Near the end of the play Macbeth says something similar, although there he speaks his real feelings (look at Macbeth's soliloquy in Act 5 Sc 3, starting with 'Take thy face hence').

Duncan's guards are suspected

Lennox says it appears that Duncan's guards have done the murder. Macbeth says he was so angry when he saw Duncan's body that he killed the guards. This is a tricky moment for Macbeth. The others would have wanted to question the guards. After all, the king's army has only recently fought off an invasion from abroad which was helped by traitors within Scotland. The guards might have been working for another enemy of Scotland. Macduff wonders why Macbeth should have destroyed the only way of finding out. Of course, Macbeth knows that the guards would have denied the murder because they were innocent. There was a risk that they might have been believed. Lady Macbeth faints just at the right moment, but it may be too late to save Macbeth from suspicion. This killing of the grooms is also the first sign that Macbeth is about to go his own way; this was not part of the plan!

Chaos

Malcolm and Donalbain are afraid

Malcolm

Duncan's sons Malcolm and Donalbain decide to escape in case they too are targets to be murdered next. Donalbain does not appear again in the play but he leaves with a telling remark about how there are 'daggers in men's smiles' all around them, echoing the 'fair is foul' theme of the play.

Actions and reactions

This is an impressively organised scene, with multiple entrances and exits and separate conversations, sometimes with different agendas. How much is Macbeth believed? Banquo, for instance, after a first brief reaction, speaks only once, to take a solemn vow. It is worth checking what that vow is: what does he suspect? Why does nobody pay much attention to Malcolm and Donalbain, and why do they immediately decide that they must flee? As for Lady Macbeth, she is strangely silent after the wonderfully telling, 'What, in our house!': does her well-timed faint, marked by a suitably attention-grabbing cry, convince anyone? And, if there are suspicions of Macbeth, why does no one speak out?

Act 2 Scene 4

Ross, Macduff and the Old Man discuss the current situation.

Chaos

This is another scene, like the one with the Porter, where the audience gets the chance to digest what has happened so far. Ross and the Old Man give simple, honest reactions to events and fill in the story. Stress is laid on the unnaturalness of the murder and how it has begun to poison all nature. Darkness 'strangles' the daylight, birds of prey are killed by the creatures they normally hunt, and Duncan's horses have turned wild and eaten each other.

Macbeth becomes king

Macduff joins them. In answer to questions he says that because Malcolm and Donalbain have fled, they are suspected of having paid the guards to do the murder. Ross mentions another one of the main themes in the play when he comments that people's 'thriftless ambition' will foolishly destroy and consume the very thing on which their life and future depend. Meanwhile Macbeth has hurried off to be crowned. Macduff hopes that the country's 'old robes' (King Duncan) do not turn out to 'sit easier' (be more comfortable) than 'the new' (King Macbeth).

Clothing

Clearly this is more than just a pious hope. Macduff is staying away from the coronation at Scone: he does not trust Macbeth, he will not be part of his court, but for the moment he will not speak out.

The murder of Duncan provokes wild happenings in the world of nature with storms, earthquakes and unnatural behaviour in animals. When the murder is discovered, Macbeth and Lady Macbeth try to avoid becoming suspects. Macbeth says that his life now has no meaning and that he feels cursed because the king has been murdered. It seems likely that he really means at least some of this and that he does not say it entirely for show.

Lady Macbeth drugged Duncan's guards and smeared them with Duncan's blood as they slept. Macbeth has swiftly killed them to stop them saying anything about the murder. Lady Macbeth pretends to faint when Macbeth is asked an awkward question about this.

Duncan's sons Malcolm and Donalbain decide to escape. They are afraid for their safety. When they disappear, suspicion does fall on them and it is thought that they have run away because of guilt.

Macbeth seems to have achieved his ambition when he is crowned king. The Old Man, Ross and Macduff discuss the terrible events and hope that things will now improve. Macduff says that he is not going to Macbeth's coronation but plans to go home instead. He raises the possibility that Scotland may suffer under Macbeth.

Self-test questions Act Two

Uncover the plot

Delete two of the three alternatives given, to find the correct plot. Beware possible misconceptions and muddles.

Banquo and his son Young Siward/Ross/Fleance meet Macbeth, who claims to have dreamed about/not to have thought about/to have served the Weird Sisters.

Alone, Macbeth sees a bloody crown/child/dagger and goes to kill Duncan/Banquo/Macduff. Unnerved by the sound of a bell/owl/scream, Macbeth describes the deed: he could not say 'Amen'/'God bless us'/'Murder!', has heard a voice crying 'Glamis hath murder'd Duncan/the King/sleep!' and thinks his hands/daggers/clothes will never be clean of blood. Early, the body is discovered by Lennox/Banquo/Macduff. Malcolm and his brother Ross/Donalbain/Macduff are suspicious and afraid: the heir to the throne flees to England/Ireland/Scone.

Who? What? Where? Why? How?

1 Who is on night watch at the castle, as the Act opens?
2 Who says he does not want to sleep, though tired – and why?
3 What happened during the night, according to Lennox, and according to Ross and the Old Man?
4 What vision does Macbeth see, and how does he interpret it?
5 Where do Malcolm and Donalbain escape to?
6 Where is Macbeth invested (crowned) as king – and who is notably absent?
7 Why did Macbeth kill Duncan's guards, why does he say he did so – and how does he get out of having to explain more fully?
8 Why can Lady Macbeth not kill Duncan herself?
9 How do the sounds of a bell and knocking connect in Macbeth's mind with Duncan's death?
10 How do the Porter's anecdotes reflect on the action of the play?

Who said that?

1 Who says: 'I am afraid to think what I have done;/Look on't again I dare not'?
2 Who says: 'My hands are of your colour; but I shame/To wear a heart so white.'?
3 Who says: 'In the great hand of God I stand, and thence/Against the undivulg'd pretence I fight/Of treasonous malice.' – and why is this ironic?
4 Who says: 'Adieu,/Lest our old robes sit easier than our new'?
5 Who says: 'Where we are,/There's daggers in men's smiles'?

Open quotes

Find the line – and complete the phrase or sentence.

1 'Or art thou but a dagger of the mind...'
2 'But wherefore could not I pronounce "Amen"?...'
3 'Will all great Neptune's ocean...'
4 'There's nothing serious in mortality...'
5 'Tis unnatural...'

Night moves

This Act is full of actions and images to do with sleeping, waking and wakefulness: they will become even more significant as the play goes on. Find three lines in the text on each of the following themes.

1 Sleep and death
2 Sleeplessness
3 Waking and summoning from sleep
4 Dreams and nightmares

Act 3 Scene 1

Macbeth arranges for Banquo to be killed.

Banquo suspects Macbeth

Banquo

Some time has passed and Macbeth is now king. In this short soliloquy, Banquo tells the audience that he suspects that Macbeth became king by foul means. What seems to you to be Banquo's main concern: his awareness of Macbeth's guilt or the possibility that, if the witches' predictions come true for Macbeth, they may do so for him as well?

Banquo does not suggest to the audience that he feels that he is in any danger from Macbeth and he remains loyal to him.

Macbeth invites Banquo to the banquet

Macbeth is about to arrange for Banquo to be murdered, so he obviously does not expect to see him at the banquet that evening. Notice how Macbeth is very keen to find out if Banquo's son Fleance is going riding with his father. This is because he wants both of them dead. Macbeth is afraid of Banquo because he knows too much about Macbeth's meetings with the witches. He is afraid of Fleance because Banquo's descendants are to become kings.

Macbeth

Notice how Macbeth has counted on the predictions of the witches coming true up to this point. Now he wants to prevent their prediction about Banquo also coming true.

'A borrower of the night'

Banquo's comment about 'becoming a borrower of the night', meaning he will be back late and it will be dark, comes true in a way neither he nor Macbeth expects. Banquo will indeed 'borrow' some time from the world of darkness to return and haunt Macbeth. In a similar way Macbeth has 'borrowed' from the dark forces of chaos, except that in his case he will have to repay the debt with his life.

Light and dark

Macbeth's view of Banquo

In a soliloquy, Macbeth tells the audience why he is afraid of Banquo. He says that Banquo is brave, clever and wise and that he is the only man he fears. Banquo was not afraid to talk to the witches and demanded that they tell him what the future had in store for them. Macbeth sees his time on the throne as 'barren' because Banquo's children will be the future kings. Macbeth's 'seeds' will not grow, but Banquo's will. This is a reminder that King Duncan promised to make Macbeth 'full of growing'.

Banquo

Time

Macbeth thinks that he has corrupted himself and murdered Duncan for Banquo's benefit. He has not done what he has done just for somebody else to get the rewards. Macbeth's battle with fate begins, as he decides to deliberately prevent Banquo's heirs from becoming kings.

Macbeth meets the murderers

Macbeth has recruited these murderers to kill Banquo. You might wonder why he does not do it himself – after all, he is a great warrior who is used to killing. Perhaps the answer lies in his reaction to killing King Duncan. Or it might be that he does not want to risk detection, especially as he is now keeping his intentions secret from his wife, the great organiser of such things. Maybe the reasons that Macbeth actually gives are really the true ones.

Order

Evil

The murderers say they are men enough to do anything. Macbeth compares the murderers to dogs but says that not all dogs are of equal quality. Some are pure breeds but others are mongrels, some are slow and some swift. Macbeth says that yes, the murderers say they are 'men', just as many different qualities of dogs are lumped together as 'dogs'. The murderers say they are men who are so bitter and reckless that they care nothing for life.

Who are the murderers?

They are men who (like Macbeth in Act 1) are driven by circumstances to turn criminal; they are not professional killers. They have both fallen on hard times. They thought Macbeth ('our innocent self') was to blame, but he has explained that their enemy was really Banquo: do you think this is true? Notice that his explanations occurred in a previous meeting. He only has to refer to that meeting, so Shakespeare maintains the momentum of the drama.

Act 3 Scene 2

Macbeth and Lady Macbeth are fearful about the future. Macbeth has a secret plan to solve their problems.

'Naught's had, all's spent'

L.M + M feel that nothing is gained → used up all their energy.

Lady Macbeth is very uneasy and feels that nothing has been gained even though they have used up all their energy ('Naught's had, all's spent'). Her anxiety is made worse because Macbeth is keeping himself to himself instead of being with her. She tries to encourage her husband to forget the past, saying that 'what's done is done', but you can see that she is herself troubled by what has happened. Perhaps she is not a monster after all, simply a wife trying to protect, encourage and support her husband.

'Scorpions of the mind'

Banquo + fleance are still alive.

Macbeth says he is afflicted by terrible dreams. He seems almost to envy the dead King Duncan who, he says, 'sleeps well'. Although Duncan is dead, Macbeth says that at least nothing can hurt him any more. Macbeth's sleep is becoming tormented: 'O, full of scorpions is my mind'. He says this is because Banquo and his son Fleance are still alive and that as darkness falls 'there shall be done a deed of dreadful note' – but he won't tell Lady Macbeth what it is.

Sleep

Imagery

'After life's fitful fever he (Duncan) sleeps well'/Macbeth must 'sleep/In the affliction of these terrible dreams/That shake us nightly.' Again the image tells us of **Character**.

Macbeth has a secret

You might wonder why Macbeth doesn't tell his wife about his plan to have Banquo and Fleance murdered. He could be waiting until it is done so that he surprises her with what for him will be good news. Perhaps he genuinely wants her to be innocent of Banquo's murder. This could be an example of him protecting her. It could equally well be that Macbeth was badly stung by his wife taking forcible charge of Duncan's murder. This could be Macbeth's way of showing that he can still do things for himself. But then you might have expected him to carry out Banquo's murder himself. Macbeth's reasons seem ambiguous and contradictory. Make up your own mind why you think he acts the way he does.

Macbeth

From bad to worse?

Macbeth's final words in this scene are ominous and say a lot about how his mind is working. He says that wickedness grows stronger through more wickedness. It seems that Macbeth is now committed to the path of evil. Later Macbeth will say that he has gone so far along the path of evil that it is as easy for him to go on as to turn back. (Look at his speech a little before the end of Act 3 Sc 4.)

Chaos

Act 3 Scene 3

The murderers attack Banquo and his son Fleance.

Darkness falls and a third murderer arrives to join the other two. Macbeth

Light and dark

seems to trust no one. The identity of the Third Murderer is open to question ('the perfect spy o' the time', referred to in Scene 1, perhaps), but you should note how he takes charge, identifying victims, assessing what is happening. This scene is full of references to darkness overpowering light, which is a metaphor for evil overcoming goodness. Just before the murder 'the West yet glimmers with some streaks of day'. Banquo and Fleance arrive with a burning torch. Banquo is murdered, but Fleance escapes. One of the murderers asks who struck out the light, which has two meanings. If you think carefully about what is said you will hear a more subtle example of this in the third murderer's comment that 'There's but one down; the son is fled'.

Order

The murder of Banquo strikes out the last glimmer of light and hope for Macbeth, but the escape of Fleance allows the witches' predictions to come true. Although 'lesser' in power than Macbeth he is also 'greater' than him in terms of goodness and future power, as Macbeth feared. Banquo's descendants will indeed become kings in spite of all Macbeth's efforts to prevent this.

Macbeth is king and he and his wife have achieved everything they wanted. They had expected to feel happy, excited and at the peak of their lives. Instead they feel threatened and unsafe. **Lady Macbeth** describes their happiness as 'doubtful'. Macbeth no longer tells his wife everything and seems to trust no one. He hires murderers secretly and even they are not trusted. He plots to kill his best friend. He still cannot sleep and his dreams torment him.

The imagery in the play begins to reflect events. Macbeth's mind is full of 'scorpions', Banquo seems to him like a poisonous snake and his life is diseased, a 'fitful fever'. These scenes take place in an increasing darkness. Macbeth talks about 'good things of day' that are overcome by 'night's black agents', and Banquo's murder happens during 'the last streaks of day'. These are symbols and images of the way Macbeth is being plunged further into evil.

Act 3 Scene 4

Macbeth holds a banquet to celebrate his coronation. Banquo's ghost appears.

The guests arrive at Macbeth's celebration banquet and are asked to take their places. At first, things seem very organised. Then the murderer arrives to give Macbeth the news that Banquo is dead, but that Fleance has escaped.

'TYRANT' is Macbeth.

The supernatural

'But now they rise again/With twenty mortal murders on their crowns,/And push us from our stools.'

Evil

Macbeth has already imagined a dagger, now he believes he sees Banquo's ghost. As with the dagger, you should think about whether these visions are caused by guilt, are a sign of his evil nature, or are sent by the witches to torment him. Or maybe he really is ill, as his guests think. Lady Macbeth again quietly accuses her husband of being a coward, as she did at the time of Duncan's murder, but apologises to the guests and covers up for him.

Chaos

Macbeth throws the calm and organised atmosphere of the banquet into turmoil in the same way as his reign as king will throw Scotland into chaos. Macbeth was probably hoping for a dignified occasion to mark his crowning, but has ended up with confusion. This is an ominous portent of the way things are generally going for Macbeth.

Banquo's ghost

Macbeth fears Banquo's ghost because it has come to accuse him of its murder.

Sleep

In the previous scene Macbeth was saying how lucky Duncan was because he was at peace in death. Macbeth had thought that the dead sleep well, but here they rise up again. So he worries that even in death there may be no peace for Macbeth. Lady Macbeth says all he needs is sleep, but this is ironic, as Macbeth 'has murdered sleep' and Banquo has risen from his 'sleep'. Macbeth did of course ask that Banquo 'fail not our feast'!

In a sense he summons Banquo's ghost: each time he sees the vision, he has just mentioned Banquo and how he misses his presence.

'Blood will have blood'

Time

After the ghost leaves and the guests have gone it is almost dawn. Night, says Lady Macbeth, is 'almost at odds with morning'. She cannot tell whether it is night or day. In their world Lord and Lady Macbeth do not know darkness from light or evil from good. Fair has become foul and foul has become fair.

Imagery

Careful examination of this scene should find no fewer than ten references to blood (or equivalents, like gore and gashes).

Chaos

In a famous speech here Macbeth talks about wading in blood. This echoes the Captain's speech about 'bathing in blood' at the start of the play and the imagery suggests similar ideas. Macbeth feels that his journey into a sea of blood has left him in so deep that he may as well hold his course now. You should consider whether Macbeth is correct or whether he could retreat from here to where he once was. In other words, how far is his fate sealed at this point?

Act 3 Scene 5

The witches meet again.

The witches

Hecat scolds the other witches for not including her in their dealings with Macbeth and says she will be with them next time they meet him. Many commentators think that this short scene was not written by Shakespeare but was added later by a lesser playwright, and some versions of the play leave it out.

Act 3 Scene 6

Lennox and another Lord discuss the terrible state of Scotland under Macbeth's rule and hope that the King of England will help them.

Order

Evil

This scene is another example of minor characters describing events so far. This helps the audience keep up to date with events that have happened or are happening somewhere else and reminds them of the important ideas in the play.

Here Lennox and another Lord discuss Macbeth's tyrannical rule and all the crimes they think he has committed in their suffering country. They hope for better times, when they might have a good king again. The first mention of English assistance comes in the news that Macduff is to plead with the English King and Seyward to help restore peace in Scotland. They want a return to a more orderly world, where there is food on their tables, where people sleep safely at night and where their feasts and banquets are freed from 'bloody knives'.

Macbeth feels confined and trapped. His one great ceremonial state occasion in the play – his banquet – is ruined because he sees Banquo's ghost.

Lady Macbeth has to take charge of him again as she did just before the murder of King Duncan. You will see that she taunts him with being a coward again, although this time she seems more weary. In contrast to her powerful speeches at the end of Act 1, here she says only that her husband needs sleep. This is the last time we see Lady Macbeth in control of events, or of herself.

This part of Act 3 is a **key turning-point** in the play. It closes the first part – Macbeth's relentless rise to power – and shows the occasion when he betrays himself. The way he talks to the ghost exposes him to suspicion, just as at the end of Act 2 when he tried to explain why he killed King Duncan's guards. Lady Macbeth pretends that he is given to fits like this. She then gets rid of their guests quickly, but she can see how far her husband has declined. Power now begins to slip through Macbeth's fingers and the second part of the action begins.

Self-test questions Act Three

Uncover the plot

Delete two of the three alternatives given, to find the correct plot. Beware possible misconceptions and muddles.

Banquo/Macduff/Malcolm suspects Macbeth of treachery. Macbeth, meanwhile, fears Banquo's/Macduff's/Malcolm's 'royalty of nature' and can't bear the thought that he has given his soul to the devil/enemy/common man so that another's heirs should be kings. He employs one/two/three murderers to kill Banquo, applauding/telling/not telling Lady Macbeth beforehand. Fleance/Banquo/Ross escapes the attackers: even so, Macbeth thinks himself safe, until Duncan's/Banquo's/Cawdor's ghost appears and sits in Duncan's/Banquo's/Macbeth's place at the feast. No-one else/everyone else/only the Macbeths can see the ghost: Lady Macbeth passes off her husband's wild behaviour as drunkenness/mirth/a fit. The witches' mistress Hecate/Acheron/Lady Macbeth plots further. Meanwhile, the Lords call Macbeth 'pitied'/'tyrant'/'butcher'. Donalbain/Fleance/Macduff is 'in disgrace' and has gone to England. War is in the air.

Who? What? Where? Why? How?

1. Who is said (slightly cynically) to be suspected of Banquo's murder, and why?
2. Who is charged to 'fail not our feast' – and why is this ironic?
3. What empty signs of kingship have been given to Macbeth if Banquo's son lives?
4. What is life in Scotland like under Macbeth's kingship?
5. Where is Macduff, where is he not (which gets him into trouble) and what is he doing?
6. Where is everyone when Banquo is attacked?
7. Why does Macbeth not sit down when invited to do so by Ross at the feast?
8. Why does Macbeth envy Duncan?
9. How does Macbeth justify the attack on Banquo to himself, and to the murderers?
10. How does Banquo deal with the witches' prophecy?

Who said that?

1 Who says: 'I am reckless what/I do to spite the world'?
2 Who says: 'Things bad begun make strong themselves by ill'?
3 Who says: 'It will have blood. They say blood will have blood'?
4 Who says: 'He shall spurn fate, scorn death and bear/His hopes 'bove wisdom, grace and fear' – and of whom?
5 Who says: 'You have displac'd the mirth, broke the good meeting,/With most admir'd disorder' – and why is this striking?

Open quotes

Find the line – and complete the phrase or sentence.

1 'Thou hast it now...'
2 'To be thus is nothing...'
3 'Naught's had, all's spent...'
4 'I am in blood/Stepped in so far...'
5 'Better be with the dead...'

Parallel lines

In a play full of prophecies, ironies and images, you'll find many echoes. Where do you find an echo of the following lines from earlier Acts of the play – and what effect is created?

1 Macbeth says: 'If 'twere done when 'tis done...'
2 Macbeth says: 'False face must hide what the false heart doth know.'
3 Lady Macbeth says: 'Tis the eye of childhood/That fears a painted devil.'
4 Macbeth is asked: 'Are you a man?' and replies 'I dare do all that may become a man.'
5 Sleep is referred to as 'great nature's second course,/Chief nourisher in life's feast'.
6 It is reported of Macbeth and Banquo that they acted as if 'they meant to bathe in reeking wounds'.
7 Macduff, finding Duncan's body, cries: 'Banquo! As from your graves rise up and walk like sprites.'

Creature features?

You may already have noticed the animal imagery in the play, particularly the poisonous and nocturnal creatures associated with Macbeth's deeds, and the owl shrieking in the night. Here are some more.

1 Of what does Macbeth take dogs as an example?
2 What dark creatures are mentioned in Scene 2 by Macbeth?
3 Who is the 'worm' that 'Hath nature that in time will venom breed,/No teeth for the present'?
4 What exotic, ferocious beasts does Macbeth dare the spirit to manifest rather than Banquo's likeness?

Act 4 Scene 1

Macbeth goes to see the witches and is shown three apparitions and a vision of the future. He learns that Macduff has escaped to England.

Chaos

Disgusting objects are thrown into a steaming pot as the witches concoct a charm. The dismembered bits of animals and humans are symbols of the witches' destructive behaviour in the play. The witches talk all the time in rhymes, which makes everything they say sound like a magic spell being chanted.

The supernatural

The witches are only a part of the supernatural forces. Hecat and the other witches may be ignored, but not the witches' 'masters' who take the form of apparitions.

Evil

The witches' 'gruel' is also an image of formless confusion, the primaeval chaos into which the powers of evil are constantly striving to plunge creation. This reflects the Elizabethan's belief about the nature of the world and the relationship between good and evil, order and disorder.

'By the pricking of my thumbs'

The witches say Macbeth is like themselves – 'something wicked this way comes'. Are the witches right? Notice how Macbeth talks to them. He does not seem afraid as he was at first. Macbeth doesn't care how much damage or chaos he causes, he just wants to know the future. Remember Banquo's warning which Macbeth seems to have forgotten. The witches will use Macbeth's readiness to believe their predictions as a way of destroying him.

Guilt

The witches manipulate Macbeth with another set of accurate, but damning, prophecies, the first of which leads to the callous murder of the Macduffs, the others to unfounded confidence.

The first apparition – an armed head

Macbeth

The apparition is of a head wearing armour. It knows Macbeth's thoughts and tells him to beware of Macduff. Although Macbeth probably thinks that the head is a vision of Macduff, you will also see by the end of the play that it is actually Macbeth's head that has been cut off.

The second apparition – a bloody child

The apparition is of a child covered in blood. It tells Macbeth that he cannot be killed by anyone 'born of woman'.

Macduff

There are various candidates for the 'bloody child': after all, Fleance has just escaped a bloody ambush, Macduff's children are about to die at Macbeth's bidding. But, given the message he imparts, the most telling identification is with Macduff who, unknown to Macbeth, was 'from his mother's womb untimely ripped'.

The third apparition – a child crowned, with a tree in his hand

Malcolm

This apparition is of a child wearing a crown and holding a branch. This is Malcolm, who later on in the play orders his army to conceal its size by hiding behind branches from Birnam Wood. At the end of the play Malcolm is crowned king.

Time

Notice how two of the three apparitions are children. Macbeth has been afraid of children all through the play, because of what they may grow into. Notice also how desperate Macbeth is to be reassured about his future. Remember Hecate's words: 'And you all know, security/Is mortal's chiefest enemy.' (3,5).

A vision of the future – a show of eight kings, and Banquo

Macbeth

Macbeth finds his worst fears realised – his hold on the crown will be only temporary. He finds it painful to look at what the witches show him. He sees a row of kings stretching out before him with Banquo smiling and pointing at them to show that they are his descendants.

Order

The ball and sceptre that the kings hold are symbols of the future joining together of England and Scotland. What Macbeth sees in the glass (a crystal ball) is King James I and his line of ancestors. Since James I was king when Shakespeare wrote the play and was known to have a deep interest in witches and the supernatural, the play would have been a favourite of his. The first performance is supposed to have been at King James I's court.

Why is Macbeth amazed?

The witches mock Macbeth with words that should remind you of Banquo's comment when they first met the witches. The witches know how shocked Macbeth is and pretend to cheer him up with music and dancing. Then they vanish forever from the play.

The prophecies resemble those of the ancient oracles which never told lies, but often deceived. The effect upon Macbeth is that his despair deepens, but at the same time he has a desperate confidence based on his understandable misinterpretation of the words of the Second and Third Apparitions.

Macduff escapes to England

Macduff

News arrives that Macduff has fled and Macbeth is once again the man of action. Without hesitation, he commands that Macduff's castle is to be attacked and everyone in it murdered. He is now ruthless and decisive. Contrast this with his soul-searching earlier in the play.

Act 4 Scene 2

Macbeth orders Macduff's castle to be attacked. Lady Macduff and her children are murdered.

Chaos

Lady Macduff is fearful and outraged that her husband has left his family. Ross reassures her that Macduff is merely being wise, and says that the times are uncertain. His short speech stresses the deep suspicion that now runs through the land ruled by Macbeth. He says that people are afraid, as those who 'float upon a wild and violent sea' and that men are now traitors and do not know themselves. In both of his comments you should be able to see references to some of the main themes in the play, as well as to Macbeth's current state.

Ambition

After Ross has gone, Lady Macduff talks to her son about his father's absence. Their conversation is full of light-hearted jokes, but is serious underneath. They talk about traitors and whether Macduff is one, but you should notice that the boy humorously makes the point that there are more traitors than honest men. Lady Macduff has no ambition and is not interested in power. Her gentle love for her child and husband contrasts strongly with the world of Lady Macbeth and her husband.

More murders

Evil

A messenger arrives to warn Lady Macduff to run away because danger approaches. She says she has done no harm but she knows that doing harm is sometimes applauded whilst doing good is sometimes dangerous. This echoes the witches' first appearance and emphasises the way fair is foul and foul is fair under Macbeth's rule. The murderers appear and begin to carry out Macbeth's orders.

The importance of Lady Macduff

Lady Macduff, wife to Lord Macduff, appears only briefly in the play and, although she is a minor character who seems to have been created only to be murdered by Macbeth's men, she also has another role in the play. Lady Macduff is the only other female character apart from Lady Macbeth (if we exclude the witches and the Gentlewoman), and is clearly a sharp contrast to her. Lady Macduff is a loving wife and mother who is loyal to her husband and who is everything that Lady Macbeth is not. Whereas Lady Macduff has no interest in political life or the pursuit of power, Lady Macbeth has given up motherly and domestic interests entirely and sought only power.

Lady Macduff is a helpless victim of the evil and disorder unleashed by Macbeth and Lady Macbeth. She is also perceptive, for she sees the danger that her husband has left her in by going to England, whereas he seems to have assumed that she would be safe without his protection.

Lady Macduff's death and that of her son are important in the play because they are examples of the tyranny and evil of Macbeth. Unlike the previous murders, they serve no purpose. They are brutality for its own sake and mark the lowest point in Macbeth's moral decline. Their deaths also mark an important turning-point in the action of the play because it is their cruel murder that hardens Macduff's heart against Macbeth. Macduff was already convinced that Macbeth was a cruel tyrant who should be toppled from the throne, but his personal grief sets him also on the path of revenge that gives him added determination to kill Macbeth.

Act 4 Scene 3

This scene is set in England. Malcolm tests Macduff's loyalty. Macduff hears about the attack on his castle and vows to kill Macbeth.

How trustworthy is Macduff?

This important scene reintroduces Malcolm. It also shows how mistrust and suspicion have grown between people under Macbeth's rule. It starts by Macduff telling Malcolm how every morning there are new widows in Scotland. Malcolm seems worried because he knows that Macduff was once loyal to Macbeth and he has not yet been harmed by him. Malcolm would also remember that Macduff was one of those in the castle the night his father was murdered.

Malcolm's suspicions are strengthened by the fact that Macduff seems to have felt it safe to leave his family behind in Scotland. These remarks are ironic, because neither man yet knows about the murder of Macduff's family.

Will Malcolm be a good king?

Macduff

In a long conversation with Macduff, Malcolm tests his loyalty by pretending to be more wicked and cruel than Macbeth. Many of the crimes he says he would commit are things which Macbeth has already done to Scotland. Malcolm lists the qualities that kings should have. Look at each one in turn and measure Macbeth against them. You will see that there is a difference between the Macbeth at the start of the play and the person he has become now. At the end of this conversation Malcolm is sure of Macduff's loyalty.

The importance of loyalty

Order

Evil

Loyalty is an important idea in the play but unthinking loyalty to the king is not enough. Sometimes the king is a man like Macbeth. Loyalty was supposed to be to the State and to the idea of order, not just to the individual who happened to be king. Malcolm has raised an army of ten thousand men to overthrow Macbeth, so that the State can return to order. This view of order and the State was very important to the people of Shakespeare's time and this is why it plays such a big part in the story of Macbeth.

It is important for Shakespeare to establish that Malcolm will be a good king and that his is a crusade of the powers of goodness and justice against the evil tyrant that Macbeth has become.

A heavenly gift

Order

The English Doctor tells Malcolm and Macduff about the King of England and how noble and good he is. He says that the king is so holy that just by touching the sick he can cure them because he has a 'heavenly gift of prophecy', which is very different to the opposite powers of the witches. These superstitions were questioned even in Shakespeare's day, but they are used here to reinforce the idea that the rightful king was appointed by God and was a force for good, supported by the powers of heaven. Contrast the English king's healing powers with the way Macbeth cannot cure himself of his suffering. Later on, the Scottish Doctor cannot cure Lady Macbeth of her illness because it too is a sickness of the mind.

Macduff swears to avenge his family

Macduff

Time

Acting again as a messenger in the play, Ross arrives with the latest bad news from Scotland. He reluctantly tells Macduff about his murdered family. Macduff swears revenge, which in those days was thought to be a proper and 'manly' feeling.

At the start of the play King Duncan said he would 'plant' Macbeth. Banquo asked the witches to look into the 'seeds of time' and say which ones would grow and which would not. The idea that all things have a natural cycle or season is repeated here as Malcolm sees himself as the angel of death or a deadly harvester when he says that Macbeth is 'ripe for shaking' and will soon fall.

= he is ready 4 his downfall.

A unique scene

This scene is unique in *Macbeth*: it is the only one outside Scotland; it is a rare occasion for debate in a fury of action; it is the only extended examination of character not involving Macbeth. Why? To enable the contrasts already mentioned to be powerfully made? To take us away from Macbeth's self-destructive path long enough to see the forces against him gathering power? To delay the climax and let it burst on the audience with still greater force? All of these are strong reasons for including this untypical scene: can you think of any others?

Macbeth has gone to see the witches. They show him that it is Banquo's descendants who will sit on the throne. Macbeth curses the witches for tricking him. This reflects the way Scotland has declined under Macbeth's rule. The many references in this Act to trust, loyalty and betrayal underline the main theme of the play. Lady Macduff wonders if her husband has turned traitor and Malcolm mistrusts him. Then Macduff does not know what to make of Malcolm's twisting and turning as his loyalty is tested by the king-to-be.

In spite of everything, Macbeth resolves to fight on. He says that those who used to be nearest to his heart will be the first to die ('the very firstlings of my heart shall be/The firstlings of my hand'). Although he probably also means that whatever he decides in future he will do straight away – without any more hesitations – this comment is ironic because the next person to die is Lady Macbeth. To some extent it is true that she dies because of his actions and in a literal sense she murders herself. Meanwhile the army of Malcolm sets off from England to overthrow **Macbeth** with **Macduff** swearing to avenge the murder of his family. The stage is set for a final confrontation between the forces of good and evil.

Self-test questions Act Four

Uncover the plot

Delete two of the three alternatives given, to find the correct plot. Beware possible misconceptions and muddles.

Macbeth seeks out the witches, who are making a charm/gruel/broth. Challenged, they call up three/two/eight apparitions who deliver a warning against Malcolm/Macduff/Fleance, and seeming promises of invincibility: the second apparition, a child with tree/crown/blood, tells him to 'Be bloody'/'Be lion-mettled'/'Beward the Thane of Fife'. Then the witches show him eight sceptres/children/kings accompanied by Duncan/Malcolm/Banquo: enraged, Macbeth has his own family/Macduff's family/Banquo's family killed. Macduff, in England, is tested by Edward/Siward/Malcolm, and shows himself passionately loyal to Malcolm/Macbeth/Scotland. Ross/Lennox/Caithness brings the news from Fife, and a dazed Macduff vows revenge.

Who? What? Where? Why? How?

1 Who is 'bloody, luxurious, avaricious, false, deceitful,/Sudden, malicious'?
2 Who is with Lady Macduff just before she is attacked?
3 What are the 'king-becoming graces'?
4 What gifts is Edward said to possess?
5 What is Malcolm's plan, when Macduff arrives?
6 Where does Macbeth meet the witches this time?
7 Why, does Malcolm imply, might Macduff still be loyal to Macbeth?
8 Why, according to Malcolm, should Macduff be generally hopeful?
9 How does Macbeth resolve to 'make assurance double sure' – and why is this ironic?
10 How many kings does Macbeth see?

Who said that?

1 Who says: 'Something wicked this way comes'?
2 Who says: 'From this moment/The very firstlings of my heart shall be/The firstlings of my hand'?
3 Who says: 'I am in this earthly world, where...to do good sometime [is]/Accounted dangerous folly'?
4 Who says: 'I would not be the villain that thou thinkst/For the whole space that's in the tyrant's grasp'?
5 Who says: 'It weeps, it bleeds; and each new day a gash/Is added to her wounds' – and of whom?

Open quotes

Find the line – and complete the phrase or sentence.

1 ' Be bloody, bold and resolute:...'
2 ' No boasting like a fool...'
3 ' Angels are bright still...'
4 ' Each new morn...'
5 ' Macbeth is ripe for shaking...'

Of woman born?

Sons are, as you may have noticed, becoming crucial to the plot. This is only one strand of an important theme in the play. Think about the following.

1 How do the 'children' of the witches' apparitions contribute to Macbeth's downfall?
2 What image of protective parenthood does Lady Macduff use – and what similar image is used later by Macduff? What does this say about them?

3 Complete the line: 'Alas, poor country/Almost afraid to know itself!...'

4 When he hears the news of his family's murder, what is Macduff's only comment about Macbeth?

5 What previous images of birth, planting and barrenness can you recall? (FIVE examples)

A matter of trust

Trust and loyalty have also become a major issue in the play by this time. Two major incidents in this Act outline the theme. Let's explore them.

1 List the three apparitions shown to Macbeth: why are they ambiguous or 'equivocal'?

2 Who says of the witches: 'damn'd all those that trust them!' and why is this ironic?

3 Who implies that Macduff is a traitor, and why?

4 Who is a 'child of integrity'?

5 Why is Macduff confused by Malcolm's confession – and whose situation does this echo?

Act 5 Scene 1

Whilst she is sleepwalking Lady Macbeth gives away secrets about the murders of Duncan and Macduff's family.

The sleepwalking scene

Several characters have complained of dreadful nightmares, and sleeplessness has been a common theme in the play. Lady Macbeth has not until now seemed bothered by bad dreams, unlike her husband whose sleep has been wrecked by them. The doctor says that Lady Macbeth's eyes are open but the gentlewoman says that 'their sense are shut', meaning that she is unconscious. You might think about whether, in a way, this has not been true all along.

Sleep

Light and dark

Now Lady Macbeth spends her nights wandering about in the darkness – literally a lost soul. She is afraid of the darkness now, perhaps in more senses than one.

Characters, Guilt, Imagery

Lady Macbeth's mental collapse is caused by her secret acknowledgement of her share of guilt and expressed once again by the blood image.

'Here's a spot'

Lady Macbeth cannot wash out the spots of blood, although after Duncan's murder you will remember her saying to Macbeth that a little water would wipe away all trace of the murder. At the time the play was written, people thought that witches carried the Devil's mark on their bodies somewhere, so the 'spot' could be a metaphor for this. If you read Act 1 Sc 5 again you will see that she has been linked with the witches before in the way she called up the spirits of darkness to fill her body.

Lady Macbeth

Lady Macbeth's speeches allow the audience an insight into her mental state. Here she is in her own private hell of blood, 'fog and filthy air'. She is a very different character now to the one we first met. This is not true of Macbeth because in this Act he becomes more like the decisive man of action he was when we first met him. Macbeth, although still a tyrant, does regain some dignity by the way he dies as a fearless warrior. Lady Macbeth is pitiful in contrast. Because she is not suffering from a physical illness the doctor says he cannot cure her. We do not see her again.

Act 5 Scene 2

The Scottish Lords begin to gather their army against Macbeth.

Macbeth's enemies gather

Chaos

Clothing

In this and in the following three short scenes, the action moves quickly from place to place towards the climax. Also several of the main themes in the play appear in rapid succession.

Angus says that Macbeth's title of king now hangs 'loose about him like a giant's robe upon a dwarfish thief' (clothing). Caithness says Macbeth's cause is 'distempered' meaning 'weak' because it is not properly tempered or hardened, and also meaning 'diseased' (chaos). He also talks about their army as medicine for the diseased country – 'sickly weal'. Lennox says the bloodletting – 'purge' – that is coming is needed to 'drown the weeds' (order).

Read again the section on themes and images (pp 12–15) for more detail on the themes and images in the play.

Act 5 Scene 3

Macbeth is told that the English army is approaching his castle. He asks the doctor to cure Lady Macbeth, but the doctor says he cannot.

'I have lived long enough'

Macbeth tries to reassure himself that everything could still turn out for the best, although he knows that this is really a false hope. In a short soliloquy he

Macbeth

Time

admits that by his actions he has denied himself all the good things that should come with old age, such as love, honour and friends. In spite of all the evil deeds he has done it is possible, because of Shakespeare's skilful work here, for you to feel sorry for Macbeth.

Notice Macbeth's use of imagery about withering plants and the suggestion that his growing season is ended. He seems to know that the time for his end has come. Having accepted this, he calls for his armour. Something of the warrior we first knew is reappearing, as he says he will fight until his flesh is hacked from his bones.

Lady Macbeth cannot be cured

Lady Macbeth

Now it is Lady Macbeth whose mind is in turmoil, whilst Macbeth seems decisive and firm of purpose. The doctor says that Lady Macbeth must cure herself because she is suffering from a troubled mind. Macbeth's anger at this could well be because he knows that both he and his wife are now beyond the help of this world. Only their deaths will 'cure' them. Try to decide if you are able to feel any pity or sadness for Lady Macbeth or her husband at this point in the play.

Act 5 Scene 4

The English army meets up with the Scottish Lords at Birnam Wood. They cut branches to hide their number from Macbeth.

At Birnam Wood

Order

All the nobles from earlier in the play have come together to join Malcolm's army. Their calm and determined mood contrasts with Macbeth's bouts of fury and shouting.

Act 5 Scene 5

Lady Macbeth dies. Birnam Wood seems to be moving. Macbeth vows to fight on.

Chaos

Macbeth says that once he would have been frightened by a shriek in the night. This is a reminder of the owl-cry heard at Duncan's murder. Macbeth says he cannot be frightened any more because he has seen so many horrors. At once he is startled by a cry.

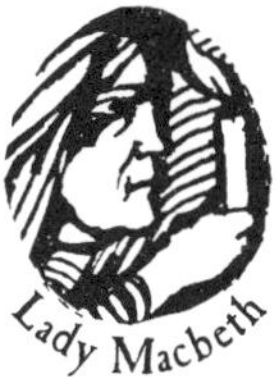

The queen dies

Macbeth seems numb at the news of his wife's death. He talks about how life seems pointless, ending only in 'dusty death'. He realises that all his efforts have been fruitless. Life is only a shadow, a fleeting thing. He says life is as meaningless as the sound and fury of an idiot's tale.

Imagery

The famous lines, 'Tomorrow and tomorrow and tomorrow...', are the finest expression of another recurring image: **Time**. Where else can you find this image?

Birnam Wood comes to Dunsinane Hill

The witches did not lie to Macbeth, but their predictions come true in a way that he could not have foreseen. It looks as if the wood is moving towards Macbeth's castle. Try to decide who you think is most responsible for Macbeth's plight – himself or the witches.

Chaos

Macbeth is weary of life, but vows to die a warrior. Throughout the play Macbeth is associated with drums, bells, alarms, storms, lightning, the screeching of wild animals and other sudden loud noises. Calling now upon the 'sound and fury' of alarm bells, storms and shipwrecks, Macbeth goes out to do battle.

Act 5 Scene 6

(In some editions this is sub-divided into 2, 3 or 4 scenes)

The battle begins and the castle is easily conquered. Macduff kills Macbeth. Malcolm is hailed as the rightful King of Scotland.

Chaos

The attacking army arrives at the castle and Macduff says the blowing of their trumpets is a forerunner to blood and death. At this point Macbeth enters, continuing the theme from the end of Sc 5. He takes comfort in the only prediction of the witches that has not yet turned against him – no man born of woman can harm him

A man not born of woman

Macbeth kills Young Seyward, but the castle is conquered. Macbeth is then confronted by Macduff, but is reluctant to fight him because of what he has already done to Macduff's family. Macbeth learns that Macduff was taken from his mother's womb early (probably a Caesarean birth) and therefore she did not bear him in the natural way. Macbeth sees that he has again been

Macduff

tricked by the witches and refuses to fight. Macduff says that, in that case, he will be tethered and put on show like a rare monster. This is too much for Macbeth, who hurls himself at Macduff. He is killed and his severed head is put on display for all to see.

Does Macbeth die nobly?

Macbeth

At the start of the play the first Thane of Cawdor died bravely and Malcolm said that 'nothing in his life became him like the leaving it'. You should think about whether this was also true of Macbeth (the second Thane of Cawdor): that he died more nobly than he lived.

King Malcolm

Malcolm

The final speech in the play comes from Malcolm, the new king, who announces that he will reward the nobles who have helped him. The imagery of planting and growing appears again. His final judgement is that Macbeth was a 'butcher' and Lady Macbeth his 'fiend-like queen'. You should look back though the play and come to your own verdict.

Your verdict

You could see Macbeth as someone who was too suspicious of those he should have trusted and too trusting of the witches, whom he should have suspected more. Or perhaps he was a terrified man trying to escape from his own conscience. Some people have seen Macbeth as a brave soldier who was also a moral coward. When making up your own mind it may help to think of how Macbeth may have been seen by Banquo, Lady Macbeth or Macduff.

Characters

Most central characters in Shakespeare at least receive a sympathetic speech on their deaths: Macbeth is a cursed usurper and a butcher. Is that the message of the entire play?

Lady Macbeth has until now always been able to dismiss from her mind the kind of images that have tormented Macbeth's sleep. She has said such things are only 'pictures' and that it is 'brain sickly' to worry about them. Now her guilt is driving her to madness whilst sleep, which she herself called 'the season of all natures', is denied to her. You will have to decide yourself whether you think her conscience might have caught up with her all at once. Maybe she didn't foresee the consequences of her deeds, unlike Macbeth who agonised about this before Duncan's murder. Because of this, some people have concluded that Lady Macbeth lacked imagination.

Macbeth has stopped thinking about the future and now looks back, perhaps with regret, into his past and thinks about the way things could have been. The great tragedy of the play is the loss of the kind of man Macbeth could have been and almost was, but for the contradictions in his character and his fatal mistake in giving in to his ambition.

In the past Macbeth has been spoken of as though he were a noble eagle or lion (e.g. the Captain reporting the battle in Act 1), but now he feels helpless, like a bear being baited.

The image of children as agents of retribution runs through the play. Duncan's child has returned to take away Macbeth's crown. Banquo's child has robbed Macbeth of the possibility that his descendants could be kings. Now the circumstances of Macduff's birth mean that Macbeth will die.

At the end of the play evil has been overthrown and natural order restored.

Self-test questions Act Five

Uncover the plot

Delete two of the three alternatives given, to find the correct plot. Beware possible misconceptions and muddles.

The doctor, after two/three/four nights of vigil, sees for himself how Macbeth/Lady Macbeth/The Gentlewoman walks in her sleep, preoccupied with a letter/the sound of knocking/blood on her hands. The English, under Malcolm's uncle/brother/father Siward, are meeting at Birnam/Forres/Dunsinane. Macbeth is aware that he is doomed/popular/unpopular, but resolute – and worries about Seyton/Lady Macbeth/Macduff. Following Macduff's/Siward's/Malcolm's ploy, Macbeth learns that Birnam Wood is burning/moving/occupied. As battle is joined, he has no time to grieve that Lady Macbeth is mad/sick/dead. We see Macbeth kill Siward/Siward's son/Macduff, before dying at the hands of Malcolm/Siward/Macduff. The play ends with the rightful king to be crowned at Scone/Colmekill/Fife.

Who? What? Where? Why? How?

1 Who refuses to fight anybody except Macbeth himself?
2 Who becomes King of Scotland?
3 What has Lady Macbeth been seen to do on previous occasions when sleepwalking?

4 What does the doctor say of Lady Macbeth's condition?
5 Where are Young Siward's wounds, and why is this important?
6 Where exactly is Macbeth's castle (previously referred to as Inverness) – and why is this significant?
7 Why, according to Macbeth, does he no longer start at the sound of cries?
8 Why is Macbeth reluctant to fight Macduff?
9 How does Birnam Wood come to Dunsinane?
10 How is Macduff able to kill Macbeth despite the prophecies?

Who said that?

1 Who says: 'Yet who would have thought the old man to have had so much blood in him'?
2 Who says: 'Some say he's mad; others that lesser hate him,/Do call it valiant fury'?
3 Who says: 'I have lived long enough. My way of life/Is fall'n into the sear, the yellow leaf.'?
4 Who says: 'Out, out, brief candle./Life's but a walking shadow'?
5 Who says: 'This, and what needful else/that calls upon us, by the grace of Grace/We will perform in measure, time and place' – and why is this significant?

Open quotes

Find the line – and complete the phrase or sentence.

1 'Here's the smell of the blood still...'
2 'And that which should accompany old age...'
3 'Tomorrow and tomorrow and tomorrow...'
4 'I pull in resolution...'
5 'And be those juggling fiends...'

Parallel lines

In a play full of prophecies, ironies and images, you'll find many echoes. Where do you find an echo of the following lines from earlier Acts of the play – and what effect is created?

1 Lady Macbeth says: 'A little water clears us of this deed.'
2 Duncan says: 'I have begun to plant thee, and will about/To make thee full of growing.'
3 Macbeth says: 'There's nothing serious in mortality – /All is but toys.'
4 Macbeth says: 'Why do you dress me in borrowed robes?'

General questions on the whole play

Using the following phrase as a memory aid (you might imagine Shakespeare shouting it, having visited his publisher...), list all the themes you can think of in the play that start with each letter.

MACBETH SOLD!

How to write a coursework essay

Most of you will use your study of *Macbeth* to write a coursework essay fulfilling the Shakespeare requirement for GCSE English/English Literature. In writing this essay there are certain requirements which must be met. In particular, you must show awareness (though not necessarily at great length) of social and historical influences, cultural contexts and literary traditions. It is also essential that you show considerable evidence of textual knowledge even if the essay has a strong creative element. Types of response might include:

- scene analysis;
- character study;
- analysis of imagery;
- empathic response to character;
- reflections on a production.

If you are writing an analytical essay, *the most important consideration* is that you must develop an argument or explain a point of view consistently throughout. There is nothing to be gained by saying what Macbeth does; what is important is that you relate his actions and words to your theme: that he is a moral coward, or is transformed by the first act of murder, or whatever else. You should make a decision on what each paragraph is about, as far as possible signalling this to the reader in the opening sentence, often called a *topic sentence* because it introduces the topic of the paragraph.

If you choose an imaginative/creative essay, *the first essential* is to reveal throughout your factual knowledge of the text and a soundly based interpretation of it. Mere imagination will not gain credit in textual study for GCSE English Literature.

The length of your essay will depend on the type of essay you write, your own wishes and your teacher's advice, but do bear in mind that it is only one of several pieces of coursework: there is no need for a 5000 word blockbuster.

Characters

You may well choose to write an essay on the characters of Macbeth and Lady Macbeth or Macbeth only. A popular and effective title is:

> *'This dead butcher and his fiend-like queen'. How far is this a fair comment on the characters of the Macbeths?*

It is important to remember that there is no 'right' answer: there are as many different views of the Macbeths as there are stage productions and literary critics. But there are some areas you must consider. Firstly, remember who says it and when: do you expect fair comment when Malcolm is looking to establish his kingdom in place of his father's killer? Secondly, you must accept that it contains some literal truth: Macbeth has butchered, or ordered the butchery, of several characters, while Lady Macbeth has often seemed in alliance with the powers of the devil (the witches). Thirdly, you will probably then feel that, for all that, it is a less than fair comment.

You will shape your essay around such considerations as the changes that occur in the characters. Look at the praise heaped on Macbeth at the beginning (surely there is some truth in that?) and the guilty collapse of Lady Macbeth (do fiends have consciences?). How much, you will ask yourself, is weakness, how much evil? Is it possible to see Macbeth as a victim of the powers of darkness?

You will also find space to consider such historical and cultural issues as belief in the supernatural, the nature of the tragic hero and, quite possibly, the fact that the presentation of Macbeth as evil is a response to James I's descent from Banquo's heirs. In fact (not that this affects your interpretation of the play) the historical Macbeth was at least as honourable a king as Malcolm Canmore and was considered to have a legitimate claim to the throne.

Macbeth and Lady Macbeth are, of course, not the only characters you could write about. However, most of the other characters might offer limited material for a full-length assignment, so perhaps you might like to group them together. You could write about what Macbeth's opponents or victims have in common, or attempt generalisations about the Scottish thanes (not just the minor characters – obviously, Macduff and Banquo as well).

Rather than a formal essay, diary or letter form can reveal character in an imaginative piece. One warning, however: evidence of detailed knowledge of the play is essential, so, though this method could explore the character of the Macbeths, Banquo or Macduff, a moving entry in Ross's diary on the dead little Macduffs is unlikely to gain much credit.

Guilt/responsibility

Whilst using much of the same material as the previous essay, this asks you to consider where to place the blame rather than exploring the main characters. A possible title would be:

Can we hold Macbeth fully responsible for the evil deeds committed in the play?

Any essay would have to conclude that Macbeth was guilty of evil deeds, many of them only hinted at in the play, as in the scene between Malcolm and Macduff (Act 4, Scene 3). It is necessary in the essay to prove his guilt, with evidence, and not simply to treat it as obvious. Then perhaps you could look at other areas of guilt and responsibility: his wife, of course, but above all the witches. It is possible to make a case for Macbeth being the victim of a concerted plot by the powers of evil (a good chance for some historical/social comments on early 17th century belief in witches and the Devil), with the witches marking him down in the first words of the play, making him dependent on them and then deceiving him. If so, does Macbeth have a case?

A popular creative essay title is:

Imagine that Macbeth was not killed by Macduff and instead stood trial for his crimes. Write an account of the trial.

Your imagination can re-create Macbeth's patterns of speech and penetrate into his thought processes, but, though you may think this more interesting than a conventional essay, it is not easier. To gain credit you must still consider the points mentioned under **Characters** and **Guilt/responsibility**, and you must make frequent and relevant reference to the text.

A potentially interesting variant on the **Guilt/responsibility** theme is to widen your scrutiny and consider why Macbeth is allowed to act as he does: what blame attaches to Banquo or Macduff or Ross and the rest for letting it happen?

The supernatural

Macbeth lends itself readily to a discussion of the supernatural, with an obvious title such as:

How significant is the role played by the supernatural elements in Macbeth?

Much of this would be straightforward: an account of the part played by the witches, with their effect on Macbeth's ambition and actions, their distinctive style of verse and their convincingly evil spells. You could start the essay as Shakespeare does the play, with the witches about to exercise their power over Macbeth, and proceed to demonstrate the significance of that power. However, there are other points for consideration:

- 'The supernatural' does not just mean the witches: there are various visions to consider, notably Banquo's ghost. Is it real? It appears on stage; the audience can see it. Is it a product of Macbeth's diseased imagination? No one else at the banquet can see it. Is it, therefore, real, but haunting the guilty murderer and only visible to him?
- The belief in the supernatural in the early 17th century is a crucial point, as well as fulfilling the need for social/historical comment. At the time to present Macbeth in the grip of devilish powers would not have been thought unrealistic.
- Macbeth's transformation of character is psychologically convincing. The supernatural powers are not imposed on him from the outside, but transform him inwardly.

- You may wish to comment briefly on the merry song-and-dance appearances (doubtless not by Shakespeare) of Hecat and the other witches.

Imagery

A particularly challenging topic would be to analyse some of the imagery in the play, possibly in general terms:

Consider the ways in which the recurring imagery within Macbeth adds to the power of the play.

Or you could concentrate on one or two of the recurring images: blood, time, light/darkness, order/chaos, etc. These images have been noted in the **Text commentary**, but you should think about how to present the essay.

Above all you should pay attention to the words 'power' and 'recurring'. It is not enough to tell us that the image is there; you must explain what effect it has. You must also show that, by constantly returning to the same image, Shakespeare builds it into the pattern of the play. Take, for instance, the 'blood' image: Lady Macbeth's mental collapse is graphically illustrated in the change from 'A little water clears us of this deed' (Act 2, Scene 2) to 'What, will these hands ne'er be clean?' (Act 5, Scene 1). In between blood has marked many things, from Duncan's servants to the Murderer's face to the Bloody Child, not to mention 'the secret'st man of blood'. And don't forget that blood also means family, descendants: the 'blood-boltered Banquo' points to kings of his blood.

Shakespeare belonged to a literary tradition of poetic drama: poetry in general depends more on imagery than prose does. Shakespeare was a poet as well as a playwright.

Be clear in your mind what various terms mean. A *simile* is an open comparison, usually using 'like' or 'as'. A *metaphor* is a concealed or implied comparison: when Macbeth is called 'Bellona's bridegroom', it does not mean that he is literally married to the goddess of war, but the comparison is only hinted at. *Imagery* is a more general term, often involving these comparisons, but including any language that summons images (pictures) to the mind and imagination of the reader or the audience.

Other topics

There are, of course, many other subjects that you could choose for a coursework essay on *Macbeth*. In particular, you could choose an analysis of a scene or a reflection on a production. If you wish to take a single scene, Act 2, Scene 2 or Act 4, Scene 1, would be good choices, but perhaps better would be to compare two scenes (early and late) for the transformation of the Macbeths.

In writing about a production, you would be expected not just to note how good (or bad) the actors were, but how the producer answered certain questions: from 'What sort of social setting?' to 'How shall I present Ross (or Seyton)?'. The most important of these questions is: 'How evil, how noble, how weak is Macbeth?'

How to write an examination essay

Most of you will study *Macbeth* as a coursework text, but it is useful to consider the approach to an examination essay on the play. Much of the advice given below will also be useful in helping you to approach any English Literature examination essays.

Before you start writing

- The first essential is thorough revision. It is important that you realise that even Open Book examinations require close textual knowledge. You will have time to look up quotations and references, *but only if you know where to look.*
- Read the questions very carefully, both to choose the best one and to take note of *exactly what you are asked to do.* Questions on *Macbeth* are likely to be on subjects similar to those considered in **How to write a coursework essay**, but you must make sure you know what is being asked: an astonishing number of candidates answer the question they *imagine or hope* has been asked.
- Identify all the key words in the question that mention characters, events and themes, and instructions as to what to do: e.g. compare, contrast, comment, give an account, etc. Write a short list of the things you have to do.
- Look at each of the points you have identified and jot down what you are going to say about each.
- Decide in what order you are going to deal with the question's main points. Number them in sequence.

Writing the essay

- The first sentences are important. Try to summarise your response to the question so the examiner has some idea of how you plan to approach it. Do not say, 'I am going to write about the character of Macbeth', but 'The phrase "this dead butcher" would seem fully justified to describe a king who causes the deaths of so many innocent subjects, but it is over-simple as an examination of Macbeth's character.' Jump straight into the essay, do not nibble at its extremities for a page and a half. A personal response will be rewarded, but you must always answer the question: as you write the essay *refer back to your list of points.*

- Answer *all the question*. Many students spend all their time answering just one part of a question and ignoring the rest. This prevents you gaining marks for the parts left out. In the same way, failing to answer enough questions on the examination is a waste of marks which can always be gained most easily at the start of an answer.
- There is no 'correct' length for an essay. What you must do is spend the full time usefully in answering all parts of the question (spending longer than the allocated time by more than a few minutes is dangerous). Some people write faster than others: they don't always get the best marks!
- Use quotation or paraphrase when it is relevant and contributes to the quality and clarity of your answer. Extended quotations are usually unhelpful and padding is a complete waste of time.

Self-test answers Act One

Uncover the plot

Macbeth, Thane of Glamis, is reported to have fought bravely against the King of Norway, and is awarded the title of the treacherous Cawdor. Returning with Banquo, he is hailed by three witches under his new title – and also as 'king hereafter': his companion is told that Banquo's heirs will also be kings. The present King Duncan invites himself to Macbeth's castle – already called a 'fatal entrance' by Lady Macbeth. Macbeth wrestles between conscience and ambition, but is spurred to action by Lady Macbeth's challenges. They will use the daggers of Duncan's chamberlains for the deed.

Who? What? Where? Why? How?

1 Malcolm; Prince of Cumberland 1,4
2 The witches 1,3
3 Thane of Glamis, Thane of Cawdor. Additionally: King of Scotland 1,3
4 Withered, wild clothes, women but bearded 1,3
5 Inverness 1,4
6 On a blasted heath 1,3
7 Because it is 'full of the milk of human kindness', and may prevent him from seizing the crown 1,5
8 Duncan is his kinsman, his king, his guest, and a virtuous man. Macbeth has been newly honoured by him, and does not want to lose his political favour yet 1,7
9 Drug them, and blame them, by using their daggers and splashing them with blood 1,7
10 Sleepless nights, and 'Though his bark cannot be lost, (Macbeth thinks he cannot be killed)/Yet it shall be tempest-tost' 1,3

Who said that?

1 Banquo 1,3
2 Lady Macbeth 1,5
3 Macbeth of Duncan 1,7
4 Duncan of the Thane of Cawdor: he is about to make the same mistake with the new Thane 1,4
5 Lady Macbeth to Macbeth, to stir him up to put his desires into bold action 1,7

Open quotes

1 'Stars, hide your fires;/Let not light see my black and deep desires.' 1,4
2 'Thou wouldst be great ,/Art not without ambition, but without/The illness should attend it.' 1,5
3 'That but this blow/Might be the be-all and the end-all here/But here upon this bank and shoal of time.' 1,7
4 'I have no spur/To prick the sides of my intent, but only/Vaulting ambition.' 1,7'
5 'We fail!/But screw your courage to the sticking-place /And we'll not fail.' 1,7

Parallel lines

1 Duncan says: 'What he hath lost, noble Macbeth hath won'. The witches can see the future 1,2
2 Macbeth says: 'So foul and fair a day I have not seen.' Macbeth is associated with the witches 1,3
3 'New honours... Like our strange garments, cleave not to their mould.' 1,3

'Golden opinion... which would be worn now in their newest gloss,/Not cast asunder so soon' 1,7
'Was the hope drunk/Wherein you dress'd yourself?' 1,7
A reminder that things are not necessarily as they seem, but can be put on and off at will

4 Macbeth says: 'Stars, hide your fires...' A hint that all signs of nobleness in him will be hidden 1,4
5 Lady Macbeth says: 'Come... unsex me here.' She is associated with the witches too 1,5

Inperfect speakers?

1 He will be lesser and greater than Macbeth, not so happy and yet happier, and the father of kings, though no king himself 1,3
2 Because we know part of the prediction has already come true, and that the witches have been waiting for Macbeth. Banquo says that their predictions 'sound so fair': how trustworthy are they? 1,3
3 That this may be an 'honest trifle' – a small piece of truth – to lead them on to betrayal 1,3
4 It cannot be ill, because there is some truth in it already, or good – because he is already horrified at how his mind is working 1,3

Self-test answers Act Two

Uncover the plot

Banquo and his son Fleance meet Macbeth, who claims not to have thought about the Weird Sisters. Alone, Macbeth sees a bloody dagger and goes to kill Duncan. Unnerved by the sound of an owl, Macbeth describes the deed: he could not say 'Amen', has heard a voice crying 'Glamis hath murder'd sleep!' and thinks his hands will never be clean of blood. Early, the body is discovered by Macduff. Malcolm and his brother Donalbain are suspicious and afraid: the heir to the throne flees to England.

Who? What? Where? Why? How?

1 Banquo and Fleance, joined by Macbeth 2,1
2 Banquo – because in repose he starts thinking about the witches' words 2,1
3 Lennox tells of storms: chimneys blown down, air filled with screams and voices, owl screeching, earth shaking 2,3; Ross and the Old Man speak of unnatural dark, an owl killing a hawk, and Duncan's horses eating one another 2,4
4 A dagger, its handle towards his hand. Either it is leading him to kill Duncan, or his thoughts of killing Duncan have produced it. (A good question to think about yourself.) 2,1
5 England and Ireland respectively 2,3
6 Scone. Macduff (who is the local Thane) 2,4
7 To prevent their denials. In a rage that they have killed Duncan. Lady Macbeth faints (pretends?) 2,3
8 Because he resembles her father in sleep 2,2
9 The bell is the summons to heaven or hell. The knocking cannot wake Duncan 2,2
10 They are about stealing, equivocating and self-destructive ambition/expectations 2,3

Who said that?

1 Macbeth 2,2
2 Lady Macbeth 2,2
3 Banquo: it is just this stand of his against pretence and treasonous malice that gets him killed 2,3
4 Macduff: the first inkling that all may not be well with Macbeth as king 2,4
5 Donalbain 2,3

Open quotes

1 'Or art thou but a dagger of the mind, a false creation/Proceeding from the heat-oppressed brain?' 2,1
2 'But wherefore could not I pronounce "Amen"?/I had most need of blessing and "Amen"/Stuck in my throat.' 2,2
3 'Will all great Neptune's ocean wash this blood/Clean from my hand?' 2,2
4 'There's nothing serious in mortality – /All is but toys; renown and grace is dead.' 2,3'
5 'Tis unnatural,/Even like the deed that's done.' 2,4

Night moves

There are lots of examples: here are just a few suggestions.

1 'The sleeping and the dead/Are but as pictures 2,2
'Sleep...The death of each day's life' 2,2
'Shake off this downy sleep, death's counterfeit,/And look on death itself!' 2,3
2 'Methought I heard a voice cry: 'Sleep no more; Macbeth does murder sleep' 2,1
'A heavy summons lies like lead upon me/And yet I would not sleep.' 2,1
'Macbeth shall sleep no more' 2,2
3 'The bell invites me...it is a knell/That summons thee to heaven or to hell.' 2,1
'Here's a knocking indeed!' 2,3
'Wake Duncan with thy knocking! I would thou couldst!' 2,2
4 'I dreamt last night of the three Weird Sisters.' 2,1
'Wicked dreams abuse/The curtained sleep' 2,1
'There's one did laugh in's sleep, and one cried 'Murder!'/That they did wake each other.' 2,2

Self-test answers Act Three

Uncover the plot

Banquo suspects Macbeth of treachery. Macbeth, meanwhile, fears Banquo's 'royalty of nature' and can't bear the thought that he has given his soul to the devil so that another's heirs should be kings. He employs three murderers to kill Banquo, not telling Lady Macbeth beforehand. Fleance escapes the attackers: even so, Macbeth thinks himself safe, until Banquo's ghost appears and sits in Macbeth's place at the feast. No-one else can see the ghost: Lady Macbeth passes off her husband's wild behaviour as a fit. The witches' mistress Hecate plots further. Meanwhile, the Lords call Macbeth 'tyrant'. Macduff is 'in disgrace' and has gone to England. War is in the air.

Who? What? Where? Why? How?

1 Fleance – because he has fled, and after all, Malcolm and Donalbain have just killed their father! 3,6
2 Banquo – because he does indeed turn up, as a ghost 3,1
3 'A fruitless crown' and 'a barren sceptre' 3,1
4 Scarce food, no sleep, violence, cutthroat politics and dishonesty 3,6
5 In England, not at the banquet, asking Edward for help to overthrow Macbeth 3,6
6 Already in the court for the banquet 3,4
7 Because he thinks all the places are full: his is occupied by the ghost 3,4
8 Because he is at rest, safe in his grave from treason, weapons, poisons and hatred 3,2
9 Banquo's honesty, courage and wisdom is dangerous: Banquo's children will rob him of the throne. Banquo is blamed for the murderers' poverty, is their enemy and Macbeth's 3,1
10 He tries to ignore it, in case his hopes are raised, which he recognises as temptation 3,1

Who said that?

1 Second Murderer 3,1
2 Macbeth 3,2
3 Macbeth 3,4
4 Hecate of Macbeth 3,5
5 Lady Macbeth: she is rarely associated with mirth and order in the play 3,4

Open quotes

1 'Thou hast it now: King, Cawdor, Glamis/All as the weird women promised; and I fear/Thou played most foully for't.' 3,1
2 'To be thus is nothing/But to be safely thus. Our fears in Banquo/Stick deep' 3,1
3 'Naught's had, all's spent/Where our desire is got without content.' 3,2
4 'I am in blood/Stepped in so far that, should I wade no more/Returning were as tedious as go o-er' 3,4
5 'Better be with the dead/Whom we, to gain our peace, have sent to peace,/Than on the torture of the mind to lie.' 3,2

Parallel lines

1 Lady Macbeth says: 'What's done is done'. Clearly, it isn't: Macbeth's fears were justified 3,2
2 Macbeth says they must 'make our faces vizards to our hearts,/Disguising what they are' A reminder of the continuing strain of deception they are under 3,2
3 Lady Macbeth says the ghost 'is the very painting of your fear'. She doesn't know that Banquo has been murdered 3,4
4 Macbeth declares 'I am a man again' and 'What man dare, I dare'. These repeated claims to manliness (rather than womanly fear) serve to raise questions about Macbeth's humanity 3,4
5 Lady Macbeth says: 'You lack the season of all nature, sleep'. She herself will fall prey to sleeplessness later in the play 3,4
6 Macbeth recognises that 'I am in blood/Stepp'd in so far'. There is a line between warlike valour and murderous butchery: perhaps Macbeth doesn't see it. 3,4
7 Macbeth wonders that 'Our graves must send/Those that we bury back.' We realise the irony in Macduff's cry: Banquo's sprite (spirit) will indeed walk... 3,4

Creature features?

1 The variety of natures called by a generic term, like 'dog'- or like 'man' 3,1
2 Snake, scorpions, bat, beetle, crow 3,2
3 Fleance – son of 'the grown serpent' Banquo 3,4
4 Russian bear, Arm'd rhinoceros, Hyrcanian tiger 3,4

Self-test answers Act Four

Uncover the plot

Macbeth seeks out the witches, who are making a charm. Challenged, they call up three apparitions who deliver a warning against Macduff, and seeming promises of invincibility: the second apparition, a child with blood, tells him to 'Be bloody'. Then the witches show him eight kings accompanied by Banquo: enraged, Macbeth has Macduff's family killed. Macduff, in England, is tested by Malcolm, and shows himself passionately loyal to Scotland. Ross brings the news from Fife, and a dazed Macduff vows revenge.

Who? What? Where? Why? How?

1 Macbeth 4,3
2 Ross – who later has to bring the news to Macduff 4,2
3 'Justice, verity, temperence, stableness,/Bounty, perseverence, courage, fortitutde.' 4,3
4 Healing and prophecy (through prayer, not divination – very different from the witches) 4,3
5 To march on Scotland with 10,000 men under Old Siward 4,3
6 In a dark cave 4,1
7 Macbeth was once honest, Macduff loved him well, Macduff has not yet been harmed by him 4,3
8 Because: 'The night is long that never finds the day' 4,3
9 By killing off Macduff's family. This doesn't make him safer from Macduff: it spurs him to revenge 4,1
10 Eight, plus 'many more' in the glass 4,1

Who said that?

1 Second witch 4,1
2 Macbeth 4,1
3 Lady Macduff 4,2
4 Macduff 4,3
5 Malcolm, of Scotland 4,3

Open quotes

1 'Be bloody, bold and resolute: laugh to scorn/The pow'r of man, for none of woman born/Shall harm Macbeth.' 4,1'
2 'No boasting like a fool./This deed I'll do before this purpose cool.' 4,1
3 'Angels are bright still, though the brightest fell.' 4,3
4 'Each new morn/New widows howl, new orphans cry.' 4.3
5 'Macbeth is ripe for shaking and the pow'rs above/Put on their instruments.' 4,3

Of woman born?

1 They give him false confidence against Macduff – who is not 'of woman born' – and against the likelihood of defeat: Birnam Wood will in fact come to Dunsinane 4,1

2 A mother wren fighting an owl from the nest. A hen with her chicks. This is a true family: the birds they associate themselves with are very different from the Macbeths' owl, crow and raven 4,2
3 'Alas, poor country/Almost afraid to know itself! It cannot be called our mother, but our grave!' 4,3
4 'He has no children' 4,3
5 Examples such as: Lady Macbeth saying she would dash her child's brains out (1,7); Macbeth saying she should bear male children only (1,7); the barren sceptre and the fruitless (childless) crown (3,1); 'I have begun to plant thee...' (1,4); 'If you can look into the seeds of time…' (1,3).

A matter of trust

1 The armed head: could be neutral, or Macduff – or Macbeth's own end
The bloody child. Encourages false security: Macduff is in fact not of woman born. The bloody child may even be a hint of this – though Macbeth takes it as a reminder to kill more children!
The child crowned, with tree. Birnam Wood will come to Dunsinane – although this sounds impossible. 'Like the issue of a king', the child may in fact represent Malcolm or Banquo's heirs 4,1
2 Macbeth. Because he has trusted them – and is damned 4,1
3 Ross and Lady Macduff: because he has left country and family 4,2; The murderers: instructed by Macbeth 4,2; Malcolm: to test his loyalty 4,3
4 Macduff 4,3
5 Because 'Such welcome and unwelcome things at once/Tis hard to reconcile.' Macbeth knows this feeling: he will be king, but his heirs will not 4,3

Self-test answers Act Five

Uncover the plot

The doctor, after two nights of vigil, sees for himself how Lady Macbeth walks in her sleep, preoccupied with blood on her hands. The English, under Malcolm's uncle Siward, are meeting at Birnam. Macbeth is aware that he is unpopular, but resolute – and worries about Lady Macbeth. Following Malcolm's ploy, Macbeth learns that Birnam Wood is moving. As battle is joined, he has no time to grieve that Lady Macbeth is dead. We see Macbeth kill Siward's son, before dying at the hands of Macduff. The play ends with the rightful king to be crowned at Scone.

Who? What? Where? Why? How?

1 Macduff 5,7
2 Malcolm 5,7
3 Walks with a candle, eyes open, writes on a paper, seals it and returns to bed 5,1
4 She needs a priest (divine) not a doctor: it is her conscience. 5,1. The patient must cleanse her own conscience 5,3
5 In the front – because this shows he has been fighting, not fleeing 5,8
6 Dunsinane – because this is in the prophecy of his defeat 5,1
7 He has 'supped full with horrors': 'direness' is familiar to him 5,5
8 Because he has shed too much of his family's blood already 5,8
9 Branches from the wood are used as camouflage for the approach to the castle 5,5
10 He was not born of woman, but was taken early from his mother's womb 5,8

Who said that?

1 Lady Macbeth 5,1
2 Caithness 5,2
3 Macbeth 5,3
4 Macbeth 5,5
5 Malcolm. It suggests that under his kingship virtue and proper order will be re-established 5,8

Open quotes

1 'Here's the smell of the blood still...All the perfumes of Arabia will not sweeten this little hand.' 5,1
2 'And that which should accompany old age,/As honour, love, obedience, troops of friends/I must not look to have.' 5,3
3 'Tomorrow and tomorrow and tomorrow,/Creeps in this petty pace from day to day/To the last syllable of recorded time.' 5,5
4 'I pull in resolution and begin/To doubt th'equivocation of the fiend/That lies like truth.' 5,5
5 'And be those juggling fiends no more believ'd/That palter with us in a double sense.' 5,8

Parallel lines

1 Lady Macbeth cannot get the stain from her hands 5,1, and Macbeth is said to 'feel/His secret murders sticking on his hands' 5,2. Macbeth was right to fear that the blood would never come off
2 The rebels have 'To dew the sovereign flower and drown the weeds' 5,2. Macbeth has grown – but, ironically, as a choking weed
3 Macbeth says: 'Life's but a walking shadow, a poor player' 5,5. Whether or not he was partly honest in his sentiments after Duncan's death, he has fulfilled his own prophecy
4 'Now does he feel his title/Hang loose about him, like a giant's robe/Upon a dwarfish thief.' 5,2. Ironically, it was Macbeth himself who first used this image of reluctance and ill-suitedness

General questions on the whole play

Here are some suggestions.

M Murder, morality, madness, medicine
A Ambition, ambiguity, animals
C Clothing, chaos, children, conscience, crown, cowardice, curse, courage
B Blood, bravery, bathing
E Equivocation, evil
T Time, trust, tiredness, tyranny
H Hospitality, hesitation, holiness, horror, health, honesty, honour, hope
S Sleep, sickness, storms, state, savagery, sleeplessness, safety, supernatural, seeds
O Order, owls
L Light, loyalty
D Deception, determination, dreams, damnation, doom, disorder, darkness, death, doubt

Notes

Notes